The Struggle for Legitimacy

CRITICAL LANGUAGE AND LITERACY STUDIES

Series Editors: Professor Alastair Pennycook, *University of Technology, Sydney, Australia*, Professor Brian Morgan, *Glendon College/York University, Toronto, Canada* and Professor Ryuko Kubota, *University of British Columbia, Vancouver, Canada*

Critical Language and Literacy Studies is an international series that encourages monographs directly addressing issues of power (its flows, inequities, distributions, trajectories) in a variety of language- and literacy-related realms. The aim with this series is twofold: (1) to cultivate scholarship that openly engages with social, political and historical dimensions in language and literacy studies, and (2) to widen disciplinary horizons by encouraging new work on topics that have received little focus (see below for partial list of subject areas) and that use innovative theoretical frameworks.

A list of all the books in this series can be found below and details of our other publications can be found on http://www.multilingual-matters.com, or by writing to Multilingual Matters, St Nicholas House, 31–34 High Street, Bristol BS1 2AW, UK.

Other books in the series

Collaborative Research in Multilingual Classrooms
Corey Denos, Kelleen Toohey, Kathy Neilson and Bonnie Waterstone
English as a Local Language: Post-colonial Identities and Multilingual Practices
Christina Higgins
The Idea of English in Japan: Ideology and the Evolution of a Global Language
Philip Seargeant
Gendered Identities and Immigrant Language Learning
Julia Menard-Warwick
China and English: Globalisation and the Dilemmas of Identity
Joseph Lo Bianco, Jane Orton and Gao Yihong (eds)
Language and HIV/AIDS
Christina Higgins and Bonny Norton (eds)
Hybrid Identities and Adolescent Girls: Being 'Half' in Japan
Laurel D. Kamada
Decolonizing Literacy: Mexican Lives in the Era of Global Capitalism
Gregorio Hernandez-Zamora
Contending with Globalization in World Englishes
Mukul Saxena and Tope Omoniyi (eds)
ELT, Gender and International Development: Myths of Progress in a Neocolonial World
Roslyn Appleby
Examining Education, Media, and Dialogue under Occupation: The Case of Palestine and Israel
Ilham Nasser, Lawrence N. Berlin and Shelley Wong (eds)
Style, Identity and Literacy: English in Singapore
Christopher Stroud and Lionel Wee

CRITICAL LANGUAGE AND LITERACY STUDIES
Series Editors: Alastair Pennycook, *University of Technology, Sydney, Australia,*
Brian Morgan, *Glendon College/York University, Toronto, Canada* and Ryuko
Kubota, *University of British Columbia, Vancouver, Canada*

The Struggle for Legitimacy
Indigenized Englishes in Settler Schools

Andrea Sterzuk

MULTILINGUAL MATTERS
Bristol • Buffalo • Toronto

Library of Congress Cataloging in Publication Data
A catalog record for this book is available from the Library of Congress.
Sterzuk, Andrea.
The Struggle for Legitimacy: Indigenized Englishes in Settler Schools/Andrea Sterzuk.
Critical Language and Literacy Studies: 12 (Settler societies and language--Looking at English language variation in schools: current & critical directions--Colonial ideologies and discourses--Constructing race in settler Saskatchewan--The racialization of space and school--Suppressing linguistic alterity in settler schools--Radical solutions for schools & teacher education.)
Includes index.
1. English language--Variation--Canada. 2. English language--Study and teaching.
3. Education--Canada. I. Title.
PE3208.8.S84 2011
427'.971–dc23 2011035421

British Library Cataloguing in Publication Data
A catalogue entry for this book is available from the British Library.

ISBN-13: 978-1-84769-518-5 (hbk)
ISBN-13: 978-1-84769-517-8 (pbk)

Multilingual Matters
UK: St Nicholas House, 31–34 High Street, Bristol BS1 2AW, UK.
USA: UTP, 2250 Military Road, Tonawanda, NY 14150, USA.
Canada: UTP, 5201 Dufferin Street, North York, Ontario M3H 5T8, Canada.

Copyright © 2011 Andrea Sterzuk.

All rights reserved. No part of this work may be reproduced in any form or by any means without permission in writing from the publisher.

The policy of Multilingual Matters/Channel View Publications is to use papers that are natural, renewable and recyclable products, made from wood grown in sustainable forests. In the manufacturing process of our books, and to further support our policy, preference is given to printers that have FSC and PEFC Chain of Custody certification. The FSC and/or PEFC logos will appear on those books where full certification has been granted to the printer concerned.

Typeset by Techset Composition Ltd., Salisbury, UK.

Contents

Acknowledgements	vii
Preface	ix

1   Settler Societies and Language   1
    Introduction   1
    Describing Racial and Linguistic Identities   3
    A Radical Counternarrative of English Language
        Variation in One Settler School   7
    Racial Domination Forged in the Past   14
    Resisting the 'Regulatory Apparatus' of Linguistics   16
    Struggling for Legitimacy   20
    Overview of the Book   24

2   Looking at English Language Variation in Schools: Current and
    Critical Directions   28
    Introduction   28
    Existing Literature on English Language Variation in Schools   29
    A Critical Direction for English Language Variation and Education   33
    Theoretical Contributions from Postcolonial Thinking   34
    Theoretical Contributions from CRT   38
    Conclusion   43

3   Colonial Ideologies and Discourses   45
    Introduction   45
    Ideologies and Discourses   46
    European Expansion and Settler Colonialism   48
    Conclusion   57

4   Constructing Race in Settler Saskatchewan   58
    Introduction   58
    A Story of Conquest and Invasion   60

     Becoming White by Learning about Others   65
     Why White Settlers Need to Dominate Others   68
     Conclusion   71

5   The Racialization of Space and School in Settler Saskatchewan   72
     Introduction   72
     East Side Meets West Side   74
     Keeping Things White: Settler Resistance to Violations of Racialized Boundaries   79
     Literacy as 'White Property'   83
     Conclusion   89

6   Suppressing Linguistic Alterity in Settler Schools   91
     Linguistic Dominance   91
     Standard Language Cultures   94
     Literacy Development   101
     Conclusion   105

7   'Radical Solutions' for Schools and Teacher Education   108
     Introduction   108
     Review of Main Arguments   108
     Implications for Schools, Teacher Education and Future Research   110

References   121
Subject and Author Index   130

Acknowledgements

This book began as my doctoral dissertation. Because of its history, many people have contributed to its writing over the years. I want to use this space to thank them here.

First, I must acknowledge the research participants who shared their stories with me. I am grateful for their generosity as well as for their trust. Thank you to Roy Lyster, my graduate supervisor at McGill University, for his mentoring and example. Without his thoughtful guidance, the academic career I have today wouldn't be possible. I wish to express my gratitude to Mela Sarkar and Teresa Strong Wilson, both members of my doctoral committee, for encouraging me through example and explicit instruction to trust my voice as a scholar and writer. I want to thank Dawn Allen, Frances Helyar, Anthony Pare, and Dana Salter for reading drafts of my dissertation as well as for their friendship. Many thanks also go out to my supportive graduate student friends at McGill: Susan Ballinger, Andréanne Gagné, and Jesus Izquierdo.

Friends, colleagues, and students at the University of Regina have also contributed to this book. I've lost count of the times that Val Mulholland has read this manuscript; given me pep talks in her office; and weighed in on decisions such as cover art. The writing of this book has also been encouraged through discussions and collaborations with Lace Brogden, Barbara McNeil, Ken Montgomery, Carol Schick, and Scott Thompson, among others. Finally, many of the ideas in this book have been worked out in lectures and discussions with my undergraduate and graduate students. I am grateful for their feedback.

Several granting agencies have supported the writing of this book both in its time as a doctoral dissertation and now as a book. I am thankful for the financial support I received from: les Fonds québécois de la recherche sur la société et la culture (FQRSC); the McGill Internal SSHRC fund; The Humanities Research Institute (HRI) at the University of Regina; and the University of Regina President's SSHRC fund.

Many thanks to Multilingual Matters and the people I've come to know through them. I'd like to thank Bonny Norton for first encouraging me to write this book. I'd also like to acknowledge the generous feedback I've received from the series editors Brian Morgan and Alastair Pennycook as well as from the anonymous reviewers.

Finally, I'd like to thank my parents, family, and friends for their unwavering support and belief in me throughout this project and my life.

Preface

In his 2008 book, *A Fair Country: Telling Truths about Canada*, John Ralston Saul provocatively claims that 'the greatest single failure of the Canadian experiment, so far, has been our inability to normalize – that is, to internalize consciously – the First Nations as the senior founding pillar of our civilization' (p. 21). The most celebrated and cherished of Canadian values, he contends – its inclusiveness, collectivism, and openness to complexity – are not a direct inheritance of European traditions but reflect, instead, a unique legacy of contact with and learning from Aboriginal peoples. Yet, such truths are rarely acknowledged for they confront the prevailing national narrative of a 'land that belonged to no one' (a *terra nullius*, in Latin), and of vast and rich natural resources that lay dormant but for the historic efforts of industrious colonizers certain in the superiority of their beliefs and abilities – and certain in their moral responsibility to civilize and guide an inferior race anchored in a universal 'pre-history'.

Fast forward to the present, as Andrea Sterzuk details in this important contribution to the Critical Language and Literacy Series, and the persistence of racist and neocolonial attitudes towards Canada's First Nations are in ample evidence – in the paternalistic accounts of welfare dependency, drug and alcohol abuse, and child neglect that surface in the mainstream media, or in the anger and impatience of white residents caught up in land claim disputes that remain unresolved due to government inaction and obfuscation. Yet, Sterzuk reminds us that such public incidents and reports, on their own, inadequately explain Canada's enduring racial hierarchy and the economic marginalization it reproduces in indigenous communities. Indeed, the foundations of inequity are deeply and systemically ingrained within nation-state institutions, one of which is education, the central focus of her illuminating inquiry.

The Canadian province of Saskatchewan, the location for Sterzuk's school-based study, is thematically resonant in several ways. Through the seizure of aboriginal lands – by force, depravation and treaty – Saskatchewan was transformed into the 'bread basket' of Canada, where poor Eastern European families were enticed by the offer of 'free land' to become commercial wheat growers (see Warnock, 2004). Sterzuk traces her own Ukrainian roots through this heroic narrative of immigrant struggle. Looking back on her prairie upbringing, she recalls the common-sense ideology of *terra nullius* that justified the dispossession of land and its transfer to homesteading families. As a teacher and educational researcher, she reflects back on the casual racism, physical and emotional segregation she witnessed, and the taken-for-granted inferiority of aboriginal values underpinned in part by school curricula in which indigenous wisdom and accomplishment were invisible or deemed irrelevant for contemporary life. When internalized by both white settler and indigenous children the outcomes of such curricula are not inconsequential to the relative high rate of school failure for First Nations and Métis students, youth unemployment and incarceration of indigenous peoples, a key argument that links classrooms and communities in Sterzuk's analysis.

In terms of schooling and invisibility, Saskatchewan also warrants mention as home to the last of over 130 federally run, Indian Residential Schools (IRS), closed in 1996 after decades of documentation showing nation-wide evidence of sexual and physical abuse of indigenous children, many of whom were forcibly removed from their families and communities based on policy goals that extended far beyond education (see e.g. Truth and Reconciliation Commission of Canada: www.trc.ca; Haig-Brown, 1988). As described by the late Cree leader, writer, and lawyer, Harold Cardinal (1999: xiv–xv), 'these schools were nothing less than state-sponsored programs of cultural genocide aimed at Indian First Nations. They were an integral component of a systematic, intergenerational, state-planned program of brainwashing aimed at removing "the Indian" from the minds and souls of Indian children'. In recent years, an official apology for the residential school system by the Government of Canada in 2008, financial compensation for the victims of the residential schools, and the ongoing hearings being held by the Truth and Reconciliation Committee, have been positive developments that acknowledge the devastating effects these schools have had on aboriginal identity in Canada and suggest more equitable indigenous–white relationships in the future.

Such positive developments, however, warrant cautious praise and critical assessment when seen though Sterzuk's de-colonial and counter-historical framework. For example, we might consider how apologies for the past also promote complacency in the present, an exaggerated confidence in the nation state's ability to correct itself by improving, rather that transforming, its existing institutional structures and values. Similarly, we might question the extent to which these shifts in policy address what Sterzuk aptly defines as 'Western cognitive imperialism' – the epistemological foundations of Canada's racial hierarchy. That is, while such public acts indicate a transition from an assimilationist to a more pluralist agenda in keeping with Canada's official multicultural policy, the depth of this shift and the substantive recognition of aboriginal difference it entails, may be partial and superficial. It may signify a growing respect for indigenous language and culture (i.e. as artifacts and folklore), but less so for indigenous philosophy, science or law in support of nation building for a highly competitive and globalized future. In this sense, the dominant society celebrates indigenous 'traditions' for their intrinsic uniqueness but also in large part for their perceived and invented obsolescence, whose reiteration serves to sustain white settler society as the 'locus of enunciation of knowledge' (Mignolo, 2010: 326) – from where truths about the imagined nation can be spoken. As Mignolo argues, 'tradition' does not precede 'modernity' but is continuously performed and positioned: an evolving dialectic of un-reason and backwardness to justify the neocolonial status quo.

Sterzuk persuasively challenges such conditions and assumptions, particularly in respect to language and schooling. In the urban school where her study takes place, and where 67% of the students self-identify as First Nations or Métis, Sterzuk provides data that indicate a prevailing standard language ideology amongst white settler teachers and administrators, against which the varieties of Indigenized Englishes spoken in the school are perceived solely as 'deficits' indicative of impoverished home environments, requiring remediation and hyper-correction. In ways that parallel a project of 'language disinvention' (Makoni & Pennycook, 2007), Sterzuk utilizes postcolonial theory to historicize and critique the neutrality and objectivity presumed around a notion of a universal, Standard English. In contrast, through observations and interviews of aboriginal teachers in the same school, Sterzuk details exemplary practices in which indigenized Englishes are validated and utilized to raise students' language awareness of the target norms expected by the school and valued in the dominant society, a pedagogical model supported by research in the interactional/intercultural work of educational researchers such as Lisa Delpit, Jim Cummins and David Corson.

Drawing on critical race theory (CRT) and whiteness studies (see e.g. Kubota & Lin, 2009), Sterzuk identifies a dominant 'colour-blind discourse' underpinning white teachers' language biases, disciplinary practices and student assessments. CRT insights are similarly foregrounded to explain several incidents at the school in which white parents question the authority and legitimacy of aboriginal teachers. In an insightful chapter on the racialization of space and schools, Sterzuk describes how white parents' resistance to aboriginal teachers and/or curricular themes could also be achieved through covert and non-confrontational means – by enrolling children in public French Immersion programmes provided in more affluent neighbourhoods away from the 'inner-city' schools where lower-class aboriginal families are concentrated and where their white, middle-class teachers refuse to live.

These types of analyses, whereby local articulations of race, class, space and time, are made explicit, illuminate the complex ways in which new, systemic forms of power/knowledge (cf. Foucault) and discrimination emerge when older ones (e.g. the Indian Residential Schools) have been officially renounced. In this respect, Sterzuk's study shares important points of reference with Roslyn Appleby's (2010) *ELT, Gender and International Development*, and the temporalized and spatialized framework Appleby deploys to illustrate neocolonial dependencies advanced through the provision of English language teaching in East Timor. Both authors, as well, utilize teachers' voices and narrative accounts in effective ways that enrich their studies and relate them more concretely to the experiences of practitioners working with similar issues and concerns.

In *The Struggle for Legitimacy*, the autobiographical voice of an experienced teacher and teacher educator is clearly present throughout and especially evident in the pedagogical suggestions Sterzuk provides in the final chapter. Saskatchewan teachers need a 'counter-history' of indigenous-colonial contact, and one that challenges the common-sense assumptions (e.g. *terra nullius*) of white settler narratives and speaks openly of race, power and poverty in the formation of the province. Chapter 4 (Constructing Race in Settler Saskatchewan) serves this purpose well and offers ample references for pre-service and in-service programming. Also of crucial need, given this study's focus on language, Sterzuk advocates for increased teacher understanding of language contact, language variation and the varieties of Indigenized Englishes spoken by First Nations students. Similarly, she recommends that teachers develop critical self-awareness of their own discourse norms and how they might bias their assessment of indigenous language and texts. Towards fairer language assessment, she also suggests that teachers consult with adult members of students' speech communities – a particularly challenging and transformative notion given the history of white-indigenous relations she details. The hiring of more First Nations and Métis teachers and support staff in the schools – another key recommendation – might further such consultations and potential community partnerships.

The Struggle for Legitimacy: Indigenized Englishes in Settler Schools is a book with strong, local ties to Saskatchewan themes and histories, but it also speaks to indigenous struggles taking place on a global scale. The 'greatest single failure of the Canadian experiment' (Saul, 2008: 21) that introduces this preface is endemic to all white settler societies, as they grudgingly and incrementally reduce systemic barriers to indigenous participation. Yet these 'baby steps' of concession and tolerance fall short of a genuine partnership and openness to the Other – a dialogic openness reflected in the recent project, 'Learning to read the world through other eyes' (Andreotti & Menezes de Souza, 2008; www.throughothereyes.org.uk). Like Sterzuk, the authors of this programme invite us to unlearn and relearn our attitudes towards indigenous knowledge – to move beyond artifacts and folklore and engage with current and future global issues through wisdom subjugated but not lost. Readers will find this important book by Andrea Sterzuk making similar invitations, especially in regards to language and education. Not all will be accepted, but hopefully they will challenge and inspire our efforts.

Brian Morgan
Alastair Pennycook
Ryuko Kubota

References

Andreotti, V. and Menezes de Souza, L.M.T. (2008) *Learning to Read the World Through Other Eyes*. Derby: Global Education.
Appleby, R. (2010) *ELT, Gender and International Development: Myths of Progress in a Neocolonial World*. Bristol: Multilingual Matters.
Cardinal, H. (1999) *The Unjust Society*. Vancouver: Douglas and McIntyre.
Haig-Brown, C. (1988) *Resistance and Renewal: Surviving the Indian Residential Schools*. Vancouver: Arsenal Pulp Press.
Kubota, R. and Lin, A. (eds) (2009) *Race, Culture, and Identity in Second Language Education: Exploring Critically Engaged Practice*. New York: Routledge.
Saul, J.R. (2008) *A Fair Country: Telling Truths about Canada*. Toronto: Penguin.
Makoni, S. and Pennycook, A. (eds) (2007) *Disinventing and Reconstituting Languages*. Clevedon: Multilingual Matters.
Mignolo, W.D. (2010) Delinking: The rhetoric of modernity, the logic of coloniality and the grammar of de-coloniality. In W.D. Mignolo and A. Escobar (eds) *Globalization and the Decolonial Option* (pp. 303–368). New York: Routledge.
Warnock, J. (2004) The political economy of racism. In *Saskatchewan: The Roots of Discontent and Protest*. Montreal: Black Rose Books.

1 Settler Societies and Language

Introduction

I was recently at an academic conference where I gave a presentation related to the topic of this book: language variation and linguistic bias in settler schools. During this presentation, I referred to Saskatchewan, the Canadian province where I live, as a *settler postcolonial context*. After my presentation, another conference delegate told me that he was surprised to hear Canada described in this way. This individual's confusion over my comment might be explained from a number of perspectives. Depending on the academic focus, Canada may or may not be 'included in a list of postcolonial locations' (Moss, 2003: 4). So one possibility, in terms of explaining his surprise, is that he was more likely to think of *postcolonial* when referring to former *colonies of exploitation* like India, Singapore, Algeria, Haiti and Guyana, to name a few. In these locations, settlers consisted of a relatively small group of Europeans (administrators, merchants, soldiers and missionaries) charged with overseeing and managing the appropriation of land, natural resources and labour. In most cases, most of these Europeans eventually left and so it is perhaps more possible to think of these locations as *postcolonial*. This type of colony differs from *settler colonies* such as Canada, Australia, South Africa, Mexico, Brazil, the United States and New Zealand where large numbers of Europeans, and subsequently others, settled on land seized from Indigenous peoples and made the new settlements their permanent homes. And while a clear divide is often made between these two types of colonial contexts – colonies of exploitation and settler colonies – there is also the danger that 'too sharp a division may obscure the terrible consequences of colonialism for the Indigenous peoples in the territories settled' (Moss, 2003: 2).

It also might be possible that this individual initially believed that I might be trying to draw attention to my own experiences as a Canadian white settler. There has, after all, been some debate in the field of literary studies about Canadian white settler writers describing themselves as colonized by the British academy and canon (Hutcheon, 1994). My conference colleague's comments might also have been related to the *post* in *postcolonial*. There are those who argue that given the continuing effects of colonialism in present-day societies, *postcolonial* is a misleading term as we have not moved past the influences of these systems. Proponents of this position might prefer, instead, to speak of *colonial* and *settler societies*; *anti-colonialism*; and *decolonization* but avoid the term *postcolonial*. While I agree that colonial systems continue to operate and affect the lives of humans who live in these societies, I use the term *postcolonial* not as a temporal marker but because, as a term and as a body of academic writing, it both signals and 'calls for a major rethinking of pregiven categories and histories, a major calling-into-question of assumed givens and fixed structures' (Pennycook, 1998: 17).

There was no time to respond to my fellow conference participant's comment and so I cannot be sure as to what his particular line of reasoning was. Irrespective of his intentions, his words had the result of giving me a moment of pause because while I recognize the differences between colonialism in different locations and understand the debate over *post* as a marker of time, I see evidence of colonialism everywhere I look in my comfortable Canadian white settler existence. Some easy symbolic examples that come to mind when I think of the influences of British imperialism on my daily life include the language I speak; Queen Elizabeth II's face on the coins in my wallet; local city streets named Victoria and Albert (Spolsky, 2009); and the girl guides who knock at my door selling cookies. These examples reflect the colonial intentions for white settler societies to serve as overseas extensions and replicas of British society (Stasiulis & Yuval-Davis, 1995).

If I look to evidence of the effects of colonialism in producing societal inequity and racialized identities in Saskatchewan, the examples become more uncomfortable for me: the teacher education programme where I work consisting almost exclusively of white bodies (students and faculty members alike) and provincial high-school graduation rates that indicate that only 25–30% of self-identified Indigenous students graduate within three years of beginning Grade 10 as compared to 72% and 75% of all Saskatchewan students (Saskatchewan Education Indicators Report, 2008). These types of examples are indicative of the role of settler schools and teacher education programmes in producing and re-producing domination, subjugation and exclusion in settler societies. Using a term like *settler postcolonial Saskatchewan* allows me to draw attention to the continuing influence of colonialism in the schools where I conduct research as well as in the society in which these schools are located.

Settler societies like Canada were created and structured (through policies and law) as racial hierarchies and this is what they continue to produce (Thobani, 2007). The semiotic act of reading colonial symbols such as currency or street names does not require high levels of critical literacy; for most, it is easy to see how British imperialism influences these aspects of the Canadian context. It may take closer analysis to see the influence of colonialism on educational inequity of Indigenous students in settler schools. This book aims to provide this closer examination by focusing on the relationships between: colonial discourses; English language variation, racialized identities and biased educational practices of settler schools, where I have been a student, teacher and, more recently, an educational researcher.

In some ways, this book's discussion may be somewhat of a departure from typical analyses of English language variation and classroom practices. Mindful of this possibility, I will discuss the theoretical framework of my research at length in Chapter 2 of this book. First though, I want to provide direction in this introductory chapter by (a) providing a discussion of some key terms and concepts that I use in my descriptions of racial and linguistic identities; (b) situating the book's arguments through a description of the classroom-based study that is central to this book; and (c) concluding this chapter with an overview of the book's content.

Describing Racial and Linguistic Identities

Choosing the terms I use to discuss the lives of people who live in settler societies shapes the types of arguments I am able to make. Smitherman (1991) argues that reality is sociolinguistically constructed. Experiences do not exist in raw or unaffected form but, unavoidably, are filtered through words. Smitherman contends that language is a key component in the development of 'ideology, consciousness, and class relations' (Smitherman, 1991: 4). What this means, in terms of the racial, ethnic and linguistic labels that I use through this book is that the words that I use are not simply neutral linguistic indicators, and so it is important to choose my words wisely as well as to share with readers the reasons behind my choices. Let me begin by describing one that I use throughout this book: *white settler society*. But what is a *white settler society* exactly? Sherene Razack describes this construct in the following way:

> A white settler society is one established by Europeans on non-European soil. Its origins lie in the dispossession and near extermination of Indigenous populations by conquering Europeans. As it evolves, a white settler society continues to be structured by a racial hierarchy. In the

national mythologies of such structures, it is believed that white peoples came first and that it is they who principally developed the land; Aboriginal peoples are presumed to be mostly dead or assimilated. European settlers thus *become* the original inhabitants and the group most entitled to the fruits of citizenship. A quintessential feature of white settler mythologies is, therefore, the disavowal of conquest, genocide, slavery, and the exploitation of the labour of people of colour. In North America, it is still the case that European conquest and colonization are often denied, largely through the fantasy that North America was peacefully settled and not colonized. (Razack, 2002: 2)

It does not necessarily sound like a great place. It is also sometimes hard to reconcile the above description with how places such as Canada, Australia and New Zealand are represented to the rest of the world and to ourselves. This is partly because a society with origins such as these produces ideologies that circulate and construct the daily lives of its racialized inhabitants long after the initial invasion of the non-European soil; the mechanisms of this process are discussed at length in Chapter 3. These ideologies have the potential to allow white settlers to view their societies as 'multicultural' and to enjoy shared stories of 'coming over', 'settling' and 'hard work'. This book suggests that these white settler mythologies, as well as how they serve to construct racialized identities, are part of the problem when it comes to determining whose languages and language varieties are allowed in official spaces like schools. As such, my use of the term *settler* when referring to individuals or groups for whom a settler society is not an ancestral home; *white settler* when referring specifically to settlers of European descent and *white settler society* to describe societies established on non-European soil by Europeans draws attention to the many complexities described by Razack in the above quotation. This decision is based on my desire to highlight the continuing role of colonialism in creating racial (and linguistic) hierarchies in settler nation-states and within the school and community where I conducted my research.

Colonialism positions white settlers at the top of a racial hierarchy. We occupy a place of dominance, not necessarily through our individual choices but through the processes and institutions that serve us. Zeus Leonardo explains this reality in the following way:

> Domination is a relation of power that subjects enter into and is forged in the historical process. It does not form out of the random acts of hatred, although these are condemnable, but rather out of a patterned and enduring treatment of social groups. Ultimately, it is secured through

a series of actions, the ontological meaning of which is not always transparent to its subjects and objects. (Leonardo, 2004: 139)

The unfortunate reality about growing up as white settlers in Saskatchewan is that colonial discourses about First Nations and Métis come to seem 'normal' to many of us at a very young age even though the processes by which this dominant identity is secured 'is not always transparent' to us. Here in the Canadian Prairies, as Epp (2008: 127) explains, 'the casual racism of everyday speech is shocking to outsiders.' And while these colonial discourses are sometimes caged in some very polite and caring language (though certainly not always), the general ideas (which I will discuss at length in Chapters 3 and 4) remain the same. Through these discourses, our dominance comes to feel mundane and unremarkable.

Settlers are not the only humans who live in white settler societies. Other peoples lived in these spaces long before European invasion and continue to live here to this day. Indigenous scholars Taiaiake Alfred and Jeff Corntassel explain indigenous identities in the following way:

Indigenousness is an identity constructed, shaped and lived in the politicized context of contemporary colonialism. The communities, clans, nations and tribes we call Indigenous peoples are just that: Indigenous to the lands they inhabit, in contrast to and in contention with the empire. It is this oppositional, place-based existence, along with the colonization by foreign peoples, that fundamentally distinguishes Indigenous peoples from other peoples of the world. (Alfred & Corntassel, 2005: 597)

In the Canadian context, other terms that are used in the same way as *Indigenous peoples* include *Aboriginal peoples* and *First Peoples*. When I narrow my focus to particular Indigenous peoples, for example, if I move from talking about Indigenous peoples in Canada to talking about Cree in Saskatchewan, it is important to use more specific terms. Let me explain what I mean by flipping this conversation to a European context. Referring to all Indigenous peoples as *Indigenous* or *Aboriginal* in discussions of local contexts would be similar to knowing that someone is Dutch and yet always referring to this person as *European* and describing cultural artefacts from his community such as clogs as *European shoes*. This type of situation, of course, would be unlikely to take place. That is not to say that generalizations about Europeans are not made, but simply that we often pay closer attention to national identities than we do to the diversity that exists among Indigenous peoples. Keeping this reality in mind, it is also important to use terms that reflect the local context of the study.

The Canadian constitution recognizes three indigenous groups – First Nations, Métis and Inuit. While it does not necessarily follow that a white settler document should determine how I refer to Indigenous peoples in Canada, it can serve as a starting point for this explanation of terms. These three groups of people are separate from one another; have unique backgrounds and traits; and within each of these groups there is much linguistic and cultural diversity and variation. *First Nations* refers to specific Indigenous peoples who live south of the demarcation that traditionally separates First Nations from Inuit. Today in Saskatchewan, the primary communities of First Nations are Cree, Saulteaux, Nakota (Assiniboine), Dakota (Sioux) and Dene (Chipewyan). Next, *Métis* are descendants of unions between First Nations and Europeans. They were offspring of First Nations women and French fur traders who worked for the North West Company or Scottish and English fur traders from the Hudson's Bay Company. Finally, the term *Inuit* refers to Indigenous peoples who have traditionally lived in the Eastern Arctic region of Canada. Of these three indigenous groups in Canada, the study discussed in this book involves only First Nations and Métis participants.

Turning now to the terms I use to describe the linguistic realities examined in my study, let me begin by describing why I do not use the term *dialect* (or *non-standard dialect*; *Standard English* or *non-standard English*) and choose instead to speak of *English language varieties* or *Englishes*. The term *dialect*, and the construct it describes, makes assumptions about the place of speakers in the world. These assumptions have the potential to construct our understandings of what counts as legitimate language. Since this book intends to trouble our understanding of this very construct, it follows that alternate terminology is in order. Every human speaks a variety or version of a language and no one variety is more *standard* (in the sense of uniformity) than another even if there are particular 'rules' about how that language should be written. As such, to refer to one variety as *standard language* or simply as *language* and another as a *dialect* is to construct a false hierarchy of language varieties.

Moving away from terms like *dialect* means that *language variation* can be thought of as the range of *language varieties* that make up the spectrum that constitutes a particular language. Some varieties are closer to one another than others; the only difference between two such varieties might be in terms of some of their phonological features or lexical items. Other language varieties differ more significantly from one another and have systematic differences on phonological, grammatical, morphological and lexical levels. Some language varieties provide greater access to power but, regardless of this unearned privilege, they remain language varieties; it is not fair or accurate to depict them as *standard language* which in turn forces another unofficial variety to be thought of as a *dialect*. I also name language varieties using what could be described as postcolonial terms (or anti-colonial, depending on your thinking). As such, I might call my own English language variety a *Canadian white settler variety* or, more specifically, a *rural Saskatchewan white settler variety*. Similarly, throughout this book, I will speak of varieties of *Indigenous English*.

A Radical Counternarrative of English Language Variation in One Settler School

Much of what is reported in this book is based on a research project conducted in one settler school in the Canadian province of Saskatchewan in 2006. This qualitative study examined aspects of school life, with particular focus on language and power. Specifically, this study set out to understand adult educators' perceptions of English(es) used by First Nations and Métis children in this study and understand the influences of these perceptions on their choices around pedagogical practices. Rogers Cherland and Harper (2007) explore what the authors refer to as *advocacy research* in literacy education. The authors describe such research as being concerned with social justice, equity and democracy with the larger goal of social transformation – the research project I describe in this book falls into this domain.

Rogers Cherland and Harper's book divides advocacy research into four categories: (a) critical literacy(ies), which draws on the work of Paulo Freire; (b) radical counternarratives in literacy research, which draw on feminist, queer, postcolonial and critical race theory (CRT); (c) literacy as social practice which includes approaches such as situated literacies, multiliteracies, adolescent literacies and activity theory; and (d) linguistic studies which they group as sociolinguistic advocacy research, psycholinguistic advocacy research and critical discourse analysis. My study explores English language variation and educator linguistic bias in one settler school and draws on postcolonial and CRT, placing it in the second category of *radical counternarratives in literacy research*. I draw attention to these categories of advocacy research because they help to describe the purposes of my research. My intent in conducting this study was not to provide a description of a particular English language variety or to determine individual educator attitudes about English language variation. Rather, this study set out to explore English language variation in one settler school from a perspective that acknowledges the persistence of colonialism in Canada; the discourses and ideologies this system continues to produce; and the impact of colonial discourses on Indigenous and settler peoples in schools.

This study took place in a settler school with an enrolment of roughly 200 students. At the time of the study, 67% of the school's population self-identified as First Nations or Métis and the remaining 33% consisted of white settlers with only a handful of settler children whose origins were something other than eastern or western European. It is also important to provide some economic facts about the school neighbourhood. Providing details about family income is in keeping with tenets of CRT (described in the next chapter), which tells us that race and the racialization of space have some very real and measurable effects on the lives of people, income is but one. Urban planning websites of 2006 indicated that the average family incomes for homes in the three neighbourhoods in which this school's students live ranged from $26,753 to $32,690. In the same year, the average family income for the city was $62,451, twice that of the research site neighbourhood.

My contact with this school was made through the use of my Saskatchewan white settler connections. A good friend I made during my undergraduate degree had a family friend who was a principal in the school division and passed my name along to the principal of the school. I draw attention to this relationship because these types of white settler networks in my province often go unnamed or unrecognized and yet they are very much a part of the social networks that elevate white settlers and that French sociologist Pierre Bourdieu would refer to as *social capital*. Elaine Smith (all participant names in this book are pseudonyms), the principal of this school, put me in contact with Deborah Desjarlais, the main classroom teacher of my study. I explained to Deborah that I was interested in learning more about the spoken and written English used by First Nations and Métis children in her classroom; educator views about 'proper' language; and the language and literacy practices of teachers at her school. After this outline of my research, she quickly agreed to allow me into her Grade 3/4 classroom all day, Monday to Friday, for almost four months.

At the time of the study, Deborah, who describes herself as Ojibiwe and as a speaker of Saulteaux and English, had over 10 years of teaching experience (10 years at the research site school and several years earlier in a reserve school). In terms of Deborah's English linguistic resources, I want to point out her adeptness at shifting from an indigenized variety of English to the variety deemed 'legitimate' for school. A story Deborah shared with me is illustrative of Deborah's ability to be fluid in English. Deborah and her eldest daughter were talking on the classroom telephone during a lunch break when several students were in the room. During this call, her daughter teased her about 'sounding white', something Deborah attributed to the intentional ways in which she changes her English in school (shifting from an indigenized variety of English to something her daughter identified as a white way of speaking) I also had the opportunity to witness her performing English in indigenized ways, for example, during teasing moments with her First Nations students. This shift in codes seemed to have the effect of punctuating the humour in the exchange. Finally, there were a number of occasions that I observed Deborah using Saulteaux with two of her students who understood this language. In short, I would describe Deborah as having strong intercultural communication abilities, something she modelled for students in her Grade 3/4 classroom, which included First Nations, Métis and white settler children, aged 8–10 years.

The total number of students in the classroom throughout the time that I was present was 25. This number fluctuated, however, as four students arrived later in the study and two students also left at different times of the study. In addition to my classroom observations, I conducted interviews with eight of Deborah's students: six First Nations children named Crystal (Saulteaux), Chantelle (Cree), Destiny (Cree), Danika (Cree), Starr (Cree) and Kenny (Cree) and two white settler girls named Hannah and Phoenix. Both Hannah and Phoenix were monolingual speakers of settler English. Neither of the girls talked a lot about their family's heritage in their interviews with me. Hannah mentioned that she thought her grandmother was 'mostly Scottish' and Phoenix thought that her father might be 'part Métis'. I chose to interview Hannah and Phoenix because of their resistance to playing and working with their First Nations classmates. Hannah, in particular, demonstrated an aversion to involvement with students who were not white settlers.

In an interview with Chantelle, one of Deborah's students, I asked her what she liked about her teacher. Chantelle described her teacher in the following way:

Chantelle: Um, I dunno, but she's really really nice ...
Andrea: Yeah?
Chantelle: ... and she's really really small (laughter)

The type of humour and the affection for Deborah found in Chantelle's description of her teacher is typical of the atmosphere of Deborah's classroom, which was filled with laughter at all moments of the day. In truth, it was one of the most peaceful classrooms that I have been in. One of Deborah's comments in an interview with me mirrors my impression: 'I don't feel you're doing your part as a teacher, if you don't have a bond or a foundation for your classroom then I can't see it being a productive happy place and I like them to feel safe and happy.' I did not hear Deborah raise her voice during the months that I spent in her classroom and, regardless of many of the difficult situations in which these children lived, their classroom was a place of happiness. An interview with Melissa, one of the educational assistants in Deborah's classroom, also reflects this description of Deborah's classroom:

Andrea: How do you describe Deborah's approach to discipline?
Melissa: Um, well I haven't really seen her discipline so to speak
Andrea: Why do you think she doesn't need to?
Melissa: I think that's because, I was going to say better teacher, but that doesn't sound right, she's a, just the way she comes across with the kids, more respectful, that's taught, right away from straight out, and I don't think it's tolerated at all so those kids know that coming in and so it works and from other classes, it's not taught.

Deborah had high academic and behavioural expectations of her students. She challenged them to do well and always believed that they could. She describes her expectations in the following way: 'we do work them pretty hard, that's my expectation for them and for myself.' A decision Deborah made while I was in the classroom demonstrates her belief in her student's abilities. It is also indicative of what I call Deborah's 'second job' at school – protecting herself and her students from institutional racism. In an excerpt from my interview with Larissa, a Cree educational assistant-in-training, the young woman introduces the topic in question when she raises her concerns over three of Deborah's students being routinely 'pulled out' of the classroom:

Larissa: I don't know, I never wanted to speak up because I always knew if you're not right up there with the kids, you're going to get pulled out and you're going to go into the other room then the other kids are going to know 'oh you're a little bit dumber than I am'
Andrea: Oh okay, so you're talking about the pull-outs, the kids who were pulled out
Larissa: Yeah, I think that it affects kids, like it affected me and my friends, so I think it's still going on in this school today
Andrea: So are you speaking of like Alberta and Kenny and Jake who get pulled out to work with like the TA's?
Larissa: Hmm, what do you mean?

Andrea: Well like, um, like they're pulled out, do you think that affects them? The fact that they're pulled out and have to work with TA's while the other kids are in the classroom with Mrs. Desjarlais?

Larissa: Yeah, cause I think some of the kids are labelling them, cause they're always pulled out, it's always those three and then when it's group time, they're together when we made our rocks, they were together, and maybe the other kids are thinking, 'maybe they're not the smarter kids'

The concerns Larissa raised about how the three boys were perceived by other students and how that might affect their view of self, social development and academic progress were also concerns shared by Deborah. She felt that she could better help them progress by keeping them in her class and expressed concerns over whether they were being suitably helped, or challenged, by their time spent in the resource room or working with educational assistants. As such, Deborah stopped this practice even though they had been regularly 'pulled out' of their mainstream classroom for this purpose for the previous two school years. I see this act as indicative of her commitment to challenging her students academically, her understanding of racial inequity in the school and her quiet resistance to having her First Nations and Métis students constructed as deficient learners.

For my student interviews, I was mostly interested in the language of the First Nations children and their exposure to Englishes (settler and Indigenous) and Indigenous languages. As such, I interviewed all the First Nations children in the class for whom I had parental or guardian permission. Of the six First Nations children interviewed, Crystal, Chantelle, Destiny and Danika made frequent visits (extended and short) to their families' First Nations (also known as 'reserves' or 'reservations' in an American context) or 'the rez', as they sometimes called it, while Starr and Kenny spent most of their time in an urban setting. These visits seem to impact on their experience of indigenous languages as well as the degree to which their Englishes could be described as indigenized. Heit and Blair's discussion of the spectrum of language characteristics of Saskatchewan First Nations and Métis students is useful in describing the linguistic performances of students involved in my research. The authors' discussion includes the following six possibilities: Saskatchewan First Nations and Métis students may be '(1) monolingual in an Indigenous language; (2) monolingual in English; (3) speak a dialect of English; (4) be bilingual in an Indigenous language and English; (5) speak an Indigenous language and some degree of English; and (6) speak English or a dialect of English and some degree of an Indigenous language' (Heit & Blair, 1993: 104).

My understanding of the students' linguistic resources comes from conversations with Deborah, what the children told me during interviews and some instances of Saulteaux- and Cree-use in the class. Crystal had some receptive skills in Saulteaux, likely because she had spent time living with her Saulteaux-speaking grandfather. On many occasions, I saw her able to recognize directions and respond accordingly (e.g. to sit down or to listen) if Deborah spoke to her in Saulteaux. In one of our interviews, I asked her about abilities:

Andrea: Oh okay, and I know you understand a bit of Saulteaux, do you-speak a little bit or mostly you just listen when people talk to you?
Crystal: I know what the words they say but I can't um, um
Andrea: Like you use English when you talk back to them?
Crystal: Yup

Deborah also described Chantelle, another child, as having receptive language skills in Cree. Her teacher attributed these abilities to the presence of Chantelle's Cree-speaking grandmother in her home. Chantelle confirmed her receptive skills in an interview with me but described her mother as being the person who spoke most often to her in Cree:

Andrea: Oh your mom, your mom speaks a bit of Cree to you. And do you understand her when she talks to you?
Chantelle: Sometimes
Andrea: Not always? No? Do you ever talk to her in Cree?
Chantelle: hmmm (interview notes indicate that she nods no)

Danika arrived one month into the study, having moved to Saskatchewan from the neighbouring province of Manitoba, where she had lived with her mother, to live with her grandparents. Danika was a speaker of Indigenous English and told me the following of her abilities in Cree:

Andrea: So you understand a little bit of Cree but you don't speak any?
Danika: Hmm, I know some words
Andrea: Yeah? Like what
Danika: Âstam
Andrea: What does that mean?
Danika: Ah, come
Andrea: Oh
Danika: And awas means get away (laughter)
Andrea: (laughter) that's a good word to know

Crystal, Chantelle and Danika appear to have not only mostly receptive skills in the Indigenous languages of their families but also a small vocabulary of words and useful expressions. Of all the children interviewed, it is likely Destiny who is most proficient in an Indigenous language:

Andrea: Ok, so do you speak a little of Cree?
Destiny: Hm-hmm
Andrea: Yeah, do you speak it with your family? Or do you mostly understand it?
Destiny: We speak it with my family
Andrea: You do. So with your grandma?
Destiny: Yep, she always talks it when at her house, you have to talk Cree if you go to her house (laughter)
Andrea: What does she do if you talk English?
Destiny: Huh?
Andrea: What does she do if you talk English?
Destiny: She just goes 'aah' and she walks away, she doesn't wanna talk.

Using the children's descriptions of their Cree and Sauteaux abilities as well as Deborah's understanding of their linguistic resources, Crystal, Chantelle and Danika, are best described by category 6 – 'speak English or a dialect of English and some degree of an Indigenous language' (Heit & Blair, 1993: 104). And while it is hard to know how much Cree Destiny speaks just by her brief account in my interview with her, it is likely that she falls somewhere between category 4 – 'be bilingual in an Indigenous language and English' and category 6 – 'speak English or a dialect of English and some degree of an Indigenous language' (Heit & Blair, 1993: 104). Shayla and Kenny would be best described by a combination of categories 2 and 3: 'monolingual in English' and 'speak a dialect of English' (Heit & Blair, 1993: 104). As I have explained, I actually see these categories as one and the same. Of all six First Nations children interviewed, it is likely that the four girls who spent time on their family First Nations and who had receptive skills in Cree or Saulteaux were mostly likely to perform their English in indigenized ways, though Shayla's English could also be described in this way. Of the six, Kenny was the least likely to perform English in this way, likely due to having lived with a white settler foster family for the previous six years.

Throughout the months that I spent in the classroom, I maintained a daily observational logbook in which I chronicled the development of the research project; described my impressions of student and educator interviews; and maintained observation, methodological, theoretical and personal field notes.

At times, I made a note of conversations between students and marked down features of their language. I then discussed these notes with Deborah in order to benefit from the insight she could provide into the classroom behaviour that I observed. I noted observations about her interaction with students and conversations that she and I had at different times of the day.

In addition to my classroom observations and interviews with the children, 10 school educators also agreed to participate in interviews with me after recruitment through staff meetings and by email (I interviewed all who were willing): Tom (Métis: spoke English; spoke and lost Michif as a child; and learned Cree as an adult), Deborah (Saulteaux: Saulteaux–English bilingual), Nicole (Métis and Cree: monolingual English speaker) and Larissa (Cree, Cree–English bilingual) and seven white settler educators named Rachel, Lisa, Melissa, Karen, Corinne, Elaine and Anita, all monolingual speakers of English. All of these educators grew up and lived their adult lives in rural and urban Saskatchewan except for Rachel who moved from another province to Saskatchewan in her late teens and Karen who lived in several Canadian provinces as a child and settled in Saskatchewan as an adult. Semi-structured interviews using questions adapted from Plank (1994) were conducted with educators in an effort to discern their attitudes and perceptions of language.

Racial Domination Forged in the Past

The patterns found in my field notes, combined with information extracted from my interview transcripts, are central to this book's critical exploration of English language variation in settler schools. It is important to note that I also make use of my own childhood stories in several places in this book and to provide readers with some justification of this decision. In Chapter 4, in the discussion of the construction of race through pedagogical activities and curriculum, for example, my memories are treated as a data source (Brodkey, 1994, 1996; Kamler, 2001; Le Ha, 2008). Roger Epp, a scholar of political studies, shares an anecdote about a pedagogical moment in one of his classes that is helpful in terms of explaining the usefulness of my childhood memories:

> I have taught introductory politics to Cree students at a cultural college housed in a former residential school, filled with peep holes and bad memories, where I once brought a group of uncomfortable non-aboriginal students for a joint session on 'self-government' that was a spectacular failure, a mismatch of those who had no sense of themselves as historical beings and those who did. (Epp, 2008: 126)

I share this anecdote from Epp's writings on the Canadian Prairies because his description of some of his students as not having a sense of themselves as 'historical beings' is useful for explaining the purposes of my childhood school memories. Throughout most of my childhood and adolescence, I was one of 'those' with no sense of myself as a historical or racial being. Living as a white settler in the Canadian prairies constructs you in this way. I share my stories of childhood not as a comparative study to the classroom I describe in this book, but because I want to demonstrate some of the ways in which white settler children, including those of us who become teachers, are schooled into positions of dominance, in part, through pedagogical activities and curriculum of settler schools. Using my childhood memories in this way allows me to create that understanding of my white settler child self as a 'historical being' even if I did not understand myself in that way at the time.

It does not seem possible to rely solely on the classroom study that informs this book to convey this part of my argument. For example, I cannot easily use the words of white settler teachers to argue these points because, as I have stated, part of being a white settler as we are constructed in this society involves not developing a sense of oneself as a historically constructed and racialized being. As I will argue in places throughout this book, we get to simply be 'normal', 'average' and 'Canadian'. Because of the luxury we have of not having to consider ourselves as raced, it is easy to develop a myopic view of the historical origins of domination and subjugation as well as of the very real ways that our racial identities impacts on our daily lives and the choices that we make. Because of this relationship between whiteness and forgetfulness about the past, comments about white settler identity and white settler school practices are mostly absent from the transcripts of my interviews with white settler educators and white settler students, except in terms of (a) what is not said; (b) what is masked through 'white talk' (see Seibel Trainor, 2005); or (c) in terms of expressing discomfort at the idea of describing oneself as white, as is the case with Rachel, one of the white settler teachers, in her comments below:

> I hate using that word too, I don't know why, it just bothers me to say white, I don't know, non-First Nations? I guess, families, well I know my family, I guess it would be white.

The ability to simply not think about one's race or all that this identity means for how we are positioned in the world differs from the realities experienced by the Cree and Saulteaux children and teachers who participated in my study. These individuals seem more likely to have developed an awareness of how they have been positioned in the world at a very young age. Indeed, it may be more accurate to describe them as being thrust into this awareness.

To summarize, revisiting my childhood memories is useful in terms of learning to understand white settler identity as historically, socially and pedagogically constructed. I include these stories of school because they help to demonstrate two things: the ways in which settler schools contribute to the racialization of students through pedagogical activities and the types of colonial discourses that circulate in my particular settler society. The teachers of my research project grew up in contact with these same messages and curricula. My childhood memories may help to shed some light on the ways in which educator choices and views of indigenized languages may be influenced by broader societal messages and experiences. For all the reasons discussed here, I include some of my own stories of childhood and schools in this book, to help 'explain what can be seen from [the] angle of vision' of a white settler child growing up; being racially constructed through pedagogical activities; and taking up her position of privilege and dominance in settler postcolonial Saskatchewan (Brodkey, 1994: 546).

Resisting the 'Regulatory Apparatus' of Linguistics

As I explained earlier in this chapter, no one's language is neutral or unmarked. In my study, the English of number of the First Nations children includes syntactic, morphological, lexical, grammatical and discourse features that could mark their English as belonging to a speaker of Indigenous English. For example, Chantelle conjugates 'teach' in the simple past verb tense as 'teached' in the following utterance: *'She teached me how to do my hair, hmm.'* Amber pronounces her 'th' as 'd' in the following utterance: *'And der's a, I got a friend dat's named Chastity.'* This phonological feature may reveal the influence of Cree on some Indigenous Englishes in Saskatchewan. As Heit and Blair (1993) explain, there is no distinction in Cree between sounds like /p/ and /b/, /d/ and /t/ and /g/ and /k/. While Amber does not speak Cree, the English of her family and community reveals the influence of the Algonquian language on the ways she performs English. Finally, Crystal shifts from past to present tense in the following utterance: *'So say, I went there for like 2 years, then I stay there with my grandma'* because she relies on the temporal adverb 'then' to mark a continuation of the past tense in the second half of her utterance.

Just as features of their Englishes mark these children as speakers of a particular English variety, my own English certainly reveals a few things about who I am and where I have been. My use of the term *bunnyhug* when

I speak of hooded sweatshirts is just one easy example of a lexical item that marks me geographically. Another example is my propensity to say things like *'I 'hink so'* (replacing the 'th' sound with an 'h' sound); *hunderd* (instead of *hundred*); and *'melk'* instead of *'milk'* when talking to Saskatchewan friends and family. I have also become aware that I employ a different past participle of the verbs 'to buy', 'to get' and 'to bring' in my compound forms. For example, I say things like: 'Had I known, I would have broughten, gotten, and boughten.' Until I moved to Montreal and an American friend laughed at me upon hearing me say this, I had no idea that other English speakers used these verbs differently. Apparently, my usage is an archaic form that continues to be employed in some areas of North America, which drew my attention to this feature in the English of other speakers from my rural area of Saskatchewan.

But it is also important to point out that my English is not locked into childhood patterns. A careful listener can likely hear the phonological influences of other languages I have learned or can recognize characteristics of Montreal English in my use of *cinema, pharmacy* and *terrace* (when, as my sister would point out, I 'should' be saying *movie theatre, drugstore* and *patio*) or when I tell my friends that my computer or phone is *open* instead of *on*. Each person's language variety reveals factors such as race, age, gender and social class but also stories about where she/he is from, has been and with whom she/he meaningfully interacts. Given this range of influences on our communication, it is probably not accurate to view languages and language varieties as tidily packaged into predetermined categories. Another way of thinking about it is that language is far more hybrid, evolving and speaker-derived than grammar books, teachers and academics like me might lead you to believe.

I have spent a lot of time considering whether or not to include a linguistic description of the language varieties that I refer to as Indigenous Englishes (Heit & Blair, 1993). My cognitive exercises have included questioning my suitability for this task in terms of my academic background in that I am not a linguist; considering the benefits to teachers and speech and language practitioners; and, finally, acknowledging my poststructuralist resistance to viewing language as strictly grammar derived. In the introduction to Clemente and Higgins (2008), which discusses the complexities of English in Mexico, Suresh Canagarajah addresses the use of the word *performance* in terms of how we think about language. He explains that this term 'draws attention to: playfulness, fabrication, strategic negotiation, situationally motivated shifts, multiple identities, hybridity, repertoire, irony, and paradox! It resists essentialising language or culture or grounding them in a specific identity, and defies traditional distinctions such as inner/outer, real/illusory and deep/surface' (Canagarajah, 2008: x). By using the word *performance*, it is possible to think about what playing with language means in terms of the types of identities we wish to project.

From this perspective then, Canagarajah argues that there is no need for debate regarding the existence of Mexican English. He maintains that:

> there are Mexican ways of using English. Wouldn't such accented-ness [not just in a phonological sense but in terms of the ways in which speakers play with a language so as to perform their identity] constitute an English specific to Oaxaca? Whether it is a recognisable system that can be named is not purely a linguistic or historical issue. It's not only a structure that can be described or a lengthy tradition of using the language locally that determines the outcome of this debate. There are also social considerations. Much depends on whether Oaxacans themselves perceive the reality of a language that is their own. The narratives in this book show that there is a consciousness of a unique or personal way of using English. The very publication of this book will help develop this consciousness both in that community and beyond – i.e. among linguists and practitioners elsewhere. (Canagarajah, 2008: xi)

Canagarajah's arguments are useful to me in terms of thinking about how I wish to present the ideas of this book. I think my hesitation about attempting a linguistic description of Indigenous English (or First Nations English, Algonquian English, etc.) is, in part, related to my concerns over whether or not this is a purely 'linguistic issue' and whether or not a linguistic description of Indigenous English is even necessary. After all, is it not enough to say that there are First Nations and Métis ways of using English? Is it actually necessary (or even possible) to describe the structures of this 'accented-ness?' Canagarajah also asks the following questions: 'When does one recognise certain variations from the norm as constituting an independent language variety? How much variation does a language need in order to be classified as a new system of communication?' (Canagarajah, 2008: ix). He maintains that such queries are increasingly irrelevant and that the asking of such questions reveals a structuralist bias towards languages. The stories told by participants in my book (as the following chapters will show) show that there is a 'consciousness of a unique or personal way of using English' among the Indigenous educators interviewed in my study. These educators acknowledge patterns of communication in terms of how they and their students perform English and express concern over some of their colleague's lack of awareness or attention to how some Indigenous students use English.

Another consideration in terms of how I approach this book's discussion of linguistic variation is my own racial identity. As a white settler speaker of a prestige variety of English, I wonder if I would even be capable of providing a robust and multifaceted representation of the Indigenous Englishes of students involved in my study. Most of my thoughts seem to stem from my concerns over fears that I would somehow invent or imagine linguistic or cultural difference. I feel concerned that my decision to provide linguistic descriptions of this particular English variety would be motivated by some unconscious desire to position Indigenous English as different or other so that my English variety can somehow be seen as normal and unmarked. Would approaching this book's analysis from the perspective of linguistic description make me complicit in that age-old settler activity of 'constructing Aboriginal culture' (Kouritzin, 2004: 249)? And yet, even in Kouritzin's discussion of the complexities of interpreting classroom communication patterns of First Nations and Métis children, she too acknowledges one particular First Nations' child's 'unique and personal way of using English' when she describes the child as a 'developing bilingual (standard English and a nonstandard dialect of English)' (Kouritzin, 2004: 255).

By providing readers with a sort of think-aloud protocol regarding my considerations, I am trying to demonstrate that we need to think carefully about the choices we make around interpreting intercultural communication and about describing language in fixed or predetermined ways. Makoni and Pennycook argue against this academic tradition of describing languages by explaining that:

> the problem for many languages previously dismissed as non-languages (dialects, sign languages, creoles) is that they have had to submit to the regulatory apparatus of linguistics in order to achieve the status of 'real languages'. The possibility of understanding language differently, from the local perspective of the users of the sign languages, dialects and creoles, is thereby dismissed as languages are brought into the universalist paradigm in which similarity and difference have already been assigned. (Makoni & Pennycook, 2007: 20)

In line with this argument, I choose not to submit the English performances of students involved in my research project to the 'regulatory apparatus of linguistics'. I offer a view of languages that posits that a debate over whether there is or is not Indigenous English is unnecessary because First Nations educators of this study demonstrate consciousness of their and their First Nations students' unique ways of using English. I maintain that some First Nations and Métis people perform English in indigenized and postcolonial ways just as I perform English in a way that signals my rural Saskatchewan white settler town-girl identity. There are a couple differences, though, between these performances of English. First, the Englishes of some First Nations and Métis people are *perceived* as marked, as signalled by common Saskatchewan descriptions of these English language varieties as an 'Indian accent' or 'Native accent'. In contrast, my English is *never* named, noticed or seen as anything other than 'English' or maybe 'proper English' or 'standard English' when I am within my province. The other difference between our marked Englishes is that indigenized ways of using English are not only often perceived as inappropriate (or illegitimate) for an official context like school but are also often viewed by educators as a detriment to acquiring print literacy (Heit & Blair, 1993). As such, when, James, a First Nations child from my study says the following: *'I done it wrong,'* he runs the risk of not being recognized (by teachers, teacher assistants, standardized test-makers, standardized test-givers and speech and language practitioners) as a legitimate speaker of English with 'grade-level' potential for acquiring print literacy. That never happened to my child self.

Struggling for Legitimacy

I want to include some statistics of reading literacy levels among settler students and Indigenous students that reflect the types of educational inequity that I have been hinting at so far in this chapter. The reading literacy statistics that I begin with are findings from the Canadian province where I live but they are also disturbingly similar to those from similar tests of reading literacy administered in the settler contexts of Australia and New Zealand. I include educational statistics from these countries, then, to demonstrate some of the similarities in patterns of educational inequity in settler societies.

Of all Canadian provinces, Manitoba and Saskatchewan have the largest proportions of their populations that are comprised of Indigenous peoples. The 2006 Canadian Census indicates that self-identified Indigenous peoples accounted for about 15% of the total population in both of these provinces. In Saskatchewan, the Indigenous population is also young and growing. Demographic projections by Census Canada indicate that by 2017, 37 out of 100 children in Saskatchewan (26% in 2001) could be First Nations or Métis and that the young adult population may almost double in Saskatchewan, reaching 30% in 2017, from 17% in 2001. I introduce these statistics to this discussion not because there is anything alarming about a large percentage of the Saskatchewan population being First Nations or Métis but because I want it to be clear that the linguistic bias and educational inequity that I describe in this book affects a significant and growing percentage of the population in Saskatchewan.

So what does the struggle for legitimacy in settler schools look like for Indigenous peoples in Saskatchewan? A recent study of levels of reading literacy among First Nations, Métis and settlers in Saskatchewan shows that 70% of First Nations participants and 56% of Métis participants, compared to 37% of settler participants, did not achieve the minimum level of literacy needed to 'use printed and written information to function in society, to achieve one's goals and to develop one's knowledge and potential' (Statistics Canada, 2008). Whether or not this 'minimum level of literacy' is representative of the reading literacy needs, purposes or reality of First Nations and Métis peoples is subject to debate, but these numbers do seem to point to different experiences with literacy education in Saskatchewan schools. If we take a look at scores from 2007 Saskatchewan Ministry of Education reading assessment tests, we again see evidence of educational inequity between settler and Indigenous students. These test results show that while at the Grade 4 level almost 80% of students across the province achieved the test standard of *adequacy* in overall reading comprehension, only 58% of self-declared Indigenous students achieved that standard (Saskatchewan Education Indicators Report, 2008: 58).

A report on 'Indigenous education and training' from the Australian Minister for Education, Employment & Workplace Relations reveals similar differences in terms of how settlers and Indigenous peoples experience education and literacy in schools in Australia (Department of Education, Employment & Workplace Relations, 2008). This report includes findings from the Programme for International Student Assessment (PISA), an initiative of the Organisation for Economic Cooperation and Development (OECD). Conducted in 2000, 2003 and 2006 with results published in 2008, this test assessed the reading, mathematical and scientific literacy skills of 15-year-old students in 30 OECD countries as well as 27 non-OECD (partner) countries. The goal of PISA is 'to assess how well students are equipped to participate productively and adaptively as adults in the rapidly changing world' (Department of Education, Employment and Workplace Relations, 2008: 57), thus allowing countries to determine the effectiveness of their education systems in preparing students for life outside of and beyond school.

As was the case with the two Saskatchewan statistical surveys of reading literacy, the 2006 PISA results revealed some significant differences between Indigenous and settler students in Australia. Overall, there was a difference of 81 points between Indigenous and non-Indigenous performance in the reading literacy component of the test (which consists of five proficiency levels). This difference of 81 points is equivalent to more than one reading proficiency level (73 points) on the PISA test and also equivalent to more than two years of formal schooling (so two grades). The results for reading literacy also revealed the following:

- In all, 38% of Indigenous students were unable to achieve Level 2, compared to 12% of non-Indigenous students and the OECD average of 21% (students achieving below Level 2 are described by the OECD as 'at risk of not acquiring essential life skills, partly because they do not have the foundation of literacy skills needed for continued learning and extending their knowledge horizon').
- Overall, 66% of Indigenous students, compared to 33% of non-Indigenous students and the OECD average of 43%, failed to achieve at least Level 3, the level of proficiency felt needed for lifelong learning in knowledge-intensive societies.
- A total of 3% of Indigenous students achieved at the highest proficiency level (Level 5), compared to 11% of non-Indigenous students and the OECD average of 9% (Department of Education, Employment and Workplace Relations, 2008: 58).

Similar to these results from the Australian context, a 2008 report from the New Zealand Ministry of Education interprets findings from a 2005–2006 international study called the Progress in International Reading Literacy Study (PIRLS) from a New Zealand perspective (Chamberlain, 2008). In 2005–2006, New Zealand and 39 other countries took part in this study to examine the reading literacy achievement of middle-primary school students. In PIRLS, reading literacy is defined as: 'the ability to understand and use those written language forms required by society and/or valued by the individual. Young readers can construct meaning from a variety of texts. They read to learn, to participate in communities of readers in school and everyday life, and for enjoyment' (Chamberlain, 2008: 7). The study revealed several general outcomes for settler students (referred to as *Pākehā/ European*, *Asian* and *Other* in the report) and for Indigenous students (referred to as *Māori* and *Pasifika* in the report):

- The mean reading literacy score for New Zealand Year 5 students (532) in 2005–2006 was significantly higher than the international PIRLS scale mean (500).
- There were both high- and low-achieving students in all ethnic groupings; however, the mean scores for Pākehā/ European (552) and Asian

(550) students were significantly higher than the mean scores for Māori(483) and Pasifika (479) students (New Zealand Ministry of Education, 2008: 5).

Though not included in the summary statistics, the mean score for Other students was 539, very close to the Päkehä/European (552) and Asian (550) students. These summary results tell us that as a group, on average, Māori and Pasifika scored significantly lower than New Zealand settlers as well as significantly lower than the international average. In terms of what these scores tell us about students' reading abilities, PIRLS includes four levels of international benchmarks (Advanced, High, Intermediate and Low). Students at the Intermediate level, for example, were able to accomplish the following:

- When reading literary texts, students could identify central events, plot sequences and relevant story details; make straightforward inferences about the attributes, feelings and motivations of the main characters; and had begun to make connections across parts of the text.
- When reading informational texts, students could locate and extract one or two pieces of information, make straightforward inferences from a single part of the text, and use subheadings, text boxes and illustrations to locate parts of the text (New Zealand Ministry of Education, 2008: 22).

As groups, both Māori and Pasifika students were significantly less likely than settler students (Päkehä/European, Asian and Other) to reach the Intermediate International Benchmark (i.e. achieve a score of 475 or higher) with more than two-fifths of Māori and Pasifika students scoring below this level.

The Canadian (Saskatchewan), Australian and New Zealand results described here reveal measurable differences in how Indigenous and settler populations perform on these tests of reading literacy. If we reject any possibility of a deficit model in terms of language development in Indigenous homes, these numbers tell us several possible stories about literacy education and Indigenous students in settler schools: (1) settler schools are doing something wrong in terms of providing reading literacy education for Indigenous students (and doing something right for settler students) or (2) test-makers are unable to develop and administer assessment tests of reading literacy development in unbiased ways. The analyses and findings from the study that informs this book will help to provide some insight into this complex reality. Things are bound to get complicated when they are 500 years or so in the making.

Overview of the Book

I find it useful to tackle large theoretical arguments in clearly outlined ways. Making sense of the colonial past and how it influences present-day school inequity in settler societies is a big task and it can feel overwhelming if it is not broken down into more manageable parts. As such, this book is peppered with summaries of 'main points' and 'key ideas' in effort to guide the reader through the book's arguments in as straightforward a manner as possible. The book is written in my own voice, using simple and straightforward language, and explanations of terminology are provided whenever new terms are introduced. I use first person narratives, or stories, throughout many of the chapters to build my arguments and to provide examples of theoretical ideas. I also want to mention that I am writing this book with a particular audience in mind: education students (undergraduate and graduate), educators, teacher educators and educational researchers in settler contexts. My stylistic choices, then, are deliberate; my goal is to make the ideas presented in this book accessible to a broad audience. By broad, I mean that I want scholars and practitioners at the range of levels described above to be able to make use of this book's information. If my writing is inaccessible due to a writing style that is too academic then I run the risk of excluding readers.

While I anticipate that this book will be read by those familiar with the settler context of Canada, it is also important to explain the relevance of its content for readers who are unfamiliar with the educational context I describe. That is, why might this book prove useful for a student of education or a teacher educator in Christchurch, New Zealand, for example? Every colonial situation is a little bit different from the next, and so it is not my intention to argue that the findings from my research should be generalized and considered to be true of every white settler society. There are reasons, though, as to why the findings from research conducted in one settler school in Saskatchewan are important to understand. My study provides readers with strong data that is helpful for the purposes of understanding the relationship between the racialized identities of students and teachers and educator views of language. Next, my study provides insight into schools as white spaces and what the racialization of institutional space means for those who learn and work within it. Finally, my research demonstrates the long-lasting implications of colonial discourses on what is considered 'normal' or desirable and the efforts educators and parents go to in order to reproduce this 'normal'. All of these are aspects of my work that can be useful when applied to developing an understanding of other settler colonial contexts.

I see the work of this book to be three-fold: (a) to develop awareness of the colonial past and its present-day influences on settler schools; (b) to take a close look at the effects of present-day settler nationalism on constructions of race and language in settler schools; and (c) to explore what could be done differently to lessen present-day and future educational inequity. The book consists of seven chapters. This first chapter has introduced the reader to the research study that informs this book as well as a number of key concepts and terms necessary for understanding many of the arguments and ideas presented in the chapters that will follow. In particular, I have argued the importance of a more expansive view of language. Such a view of language allows space for introducing alternative understandings of English in settler schools. In the chapters that follow, I will pull together ideas from this introductory chapter through my discussions and analysis of findings from the study conducted in the settler school context I described in this chapter.

Chapter 2 begins with a discussion of prevalent research trends in English language variation in educational contexts. This overview includes a summary and description of research trends that include research that investigates the systematicity of 'nonstandard dialects'; investigates the impact of educators' deficit views of linguistic variation; explores the influence of 'dialect interference' on the development of print literacy; examines linguistically biased assessment tools; explores the impact of 'dialect awareness;' and discusses the place of non-school-sanctioned linguistic varieties in classrooms. In Chapter 2, I make the argument that these types of localized investigations may fall short of recognizing educator linguistic bias as both socially and historically embedded. I suggest, instead, that a critical view of language variation is necessary, one that more fully considers factors such as educators' racialized identities and the historical context that produces them. I turn then to the possibilities created by drawing on postcolonial theory and CRT. Chapter 2 argues that these ideas allow for a critical analysis of language use and literacy education in a settler context; permit us to see the significance of race in a settler society; and understand the ways in which schools are complicit in the production of racial inequity. This view of English language variation as a historical and social construct creates space for issues such as colonialism, race and dominance to settle into this book's discussions.

Drawing on ideas introduced in Chapter 2, Chapter 3 uses ideas from postcolonial theory to discuss the functions of ideologies and discourses, consider European imperialism and examine colonialism and nationalism in settler societies. More than an overview of European expansion and settlement, this chapter explores the thinking that accompanies colonization through a discussion of the societal impact of ideas like *terra nullius* and *common destiny*.

Chapter 4 combines my childhood memories of school activities to create a postcolonial rendering of settler Saskatchewan history. This chapter begins with a counter-history of Saskatchewan that exposes the 'building blocks' of present-day inequity. Through the inclusion of my own school memories, I seek to compare and contrast the realities of Saskatchewan's story of invasion, settlement and dominance with how it was packaged as school units and lessons for me, as a white settler student in rural Saskatchewan. This chapter examines some of the ways that pedagogical activities serve as mechanisms in the production of societal inequity and dominant racialized identities.

Chapter 5 extends this analysis of school as a colonial mechanism to a consideration of schools and community as racialized spaces. This discussion of 'space as race' moves us beyond simply understanding curriculum as a discursive text and also allows us to understand how parents; teachers and children are involved in taking up positions of dominance and resistance. Coming to a view of schools as white spaces and curriculum as a colonial mechanism moves us towards a more critical understanding of why particular Englishes are valued in school spaces and just what lies behind school projects that seek to expel Indigenous English from the whiteness of the school space.

Chapter 6 underscores the importance of viewing the societal and school suppression of linguistic alterity as a colonial mechanism common to settler societies. Settler societies are united in the need to produce (linguistic) homogeneity in a (linguistically) heterogeneous society; these are components of the creation of an imaginary national identity. This chapter also introduces readers to standard language ideologies and discourses and examines linguistic othering as a tool used for maintaining educational (and societal) inequity between groups. Drawing on data from interviews with teachers, administrators and educational assistants, this chapter examines educator perceptions and beliefs regarding linguistic and discourse characteristics of Indigenous English as well as the print literacy development of First Nations and Métis students. This chapter reveals the ways in which educators' racial identities are implicated in their views of English as well as in their understanding of students as having (or not having) potential for successful literacy development.

This book concludes with Chapter 7 and its discussion of implications for schools, teacher education programmes and future research. The chapter is divided into two parts and begins with a summary and discussion on the findings of research as discussed in this book. The exploration of the book's main arguments moves through the following key points: an understanding that language and schooling are historically and socially located; race matters in settler societies; colonialism continues to produce us; educator linguistic bias is not simply a misunderstanding about language or practice; and schools and communities are racialized spaces as are the people who live, study and work within them. After a resume and synthesis of these mains points, the chapter concludes with a discussion of suggestions for schools, teachers, preservice teaching programmes and future research in this field.

2 Looking at English Language Variation in Schools: Current and Critical Directions

Introduction

In Chapter 1, I introduced the central goal of this book: to examine the relationship between views of English language variation in schools and societal processes such as colonialism and nationalism. As I explained, this book uses examples from a study conducted in one Canadian school to demonstrate the ways in which educator beliefs about language; educators' and students' racialized identities and experiences; and racialized spaces of schools and cities continue to produce and be produced by colonialism and nationalism in settler societies. Literature in the fields of education and applied linguistics does not always approach language variation in this way. The prevailing trend, rather, is to examine literacy practices at a local level, with a focus on perhaps the systematicity of a particular language variety; the place of 'nonstandard dialects' in schools; or the benefits of a particular pedagogical intervention, to name a few examples. Certainly, research exists which extends the analysis to include race and exclusion but oftentimes it does so without the additional step of viewing linguistic dominance as a historical construct. The critical analyses presented in this book are intended to demonstrate these links and to highlight the importance of these concepts, among others, for the fields of teacher education and applied linguistics.

I do not intend to offer the arguments of this book as a new paradigm or as a replacement for the valuable work that is already being conducted around English language variation and education. I am not the first person in applied linguistics to notice that race plays a role in matters of language (as may other factors such as gender; socioeconomic status and social status). Rather, I see the work of this book as making explicit some of the connections and possible contributions between other academic fields such as postcolonial theory and CRT and research on English language variation and schools.

Drawing on work in these academic fields systematically opens up the possibility for fully understanding the mechanisms of schools. Towards this goal, then, I have two objectives: (1) to provide an overview of some of the current and prevalent ways of looking at English language variation in schools and (2) to demonstrate how this body of literature can be enriched by drawing on ideas from CRT and postcolonial theory. This theoretical foundation, as outlined in this chapter, informs the analyses and arguments presented here and throughout the rest of the book.

Existing Literature on English Language Variation in Schools

As in the case of any area of academic interest, research on English language variation in schools covers a broad range of topics investigated using a variety of qualitative and quantitative methods. Just as the methods used to produce studies of English language variation in schools vary, so can the topics of research. For example, researchers in English language variation and schools have investigated the systematicity of 'nonstandard dialects' with an aim to reveal the rules that govern them. The general idea behind this particular area of enquiry is the argument that if an English can be demonstrated to be rule-governed and systematic, then its validity can be argued. One of the early examples of this particular type of research is the descriptive studies of urban African American Vernacular English conducted by William Labov in New York City in the late 1960s (Labov, 1972). His findings demonstrating the rule-governed nature of African American Vernacular English (AAVE) continue to influence English language variation research to this day.

Another area of investigation is research that examines attitudes, deficit views and teacher expectations of students who speak 'nonstandard dialects' as well as the types of teacher behaviours that may result from these beliefs (Aaron & Powell, 1982; Abdul-Hakim, 2002; Blake & Cutler, 2003; Cecil, 1988; Covington, 1975; Di Giulio, 1973; Ford, 1978; Goodman & Buck, 1973; Hoover *et al.*, 1996; Simpson & Erickson, 1983; Taylor, 1973; Williams, 1973; Woodworth & Salzar, 1971). Using a range of qualitative and quantitative research methods including questionnaires, surveys, interviews and matched guise tests, this body of research explores these types of beliefs and attitudes and, in some cases, also attempts to measure the relationship between teacher beliefs and student performance. The notion underlying this body of research is that proponents of a deficit view of English variation 'believe that speakers of dialects with non-standard forms have a handicap – socially and cognitively – because the dialects are illogical, or sloppy, or just bad grammar'

(Wolfram et al., 1999: 20). For example, Cecil's (1988) examination of 55 white teachers used questionnaires to examine their attitudes towards African American English. Her study found that the teachers surveyed expected significantly greater overall academic achievement, reading success and intelligence from those children who spoke 'Standard English' than from those who spoke varieties of African American English. These findings regarding biased teacher expectations are also reflected in an earlier study by Goodman and Buck (1973), which explored the influences of differences between home and school language varieties and African American English speakers' acquisition of reading. This study found that it was the rejection of the learner's language variety by educators, and not linguistic differences, which created a special disadvantage for learners.

There is also literature that explores complications created by lack of fluency in a prestige variety of language used for reading education in schools (Roy, 1987; Wolfram & Schilling-Estes, 1998). These complications are sometimes referred to as 'dialect interference'. There is, indeed, a relationship between spoken and written language and print literacy needs to be considered in relation to the oral mastery of a language. That is, literacy is not so much a skill to be acquired as it is a system that exploits and elaborates a person's knowledge of spoken language. This argument claims that it is lack of fluency in the school-sanctioned variety of English that causes interruptions and delays in students' mastery of literacy skills and, subsequently, subject matter. Children who speak varieties of English with features that differ from the norms of written language commonly used in literacy education do not automatically become fluent in this new school-sanctioned variety on entering kindergarten (Roy, 1987). Many linguists, teachers and educational researchers who understand the relationship between spoken and written language argue that fluency of this kind can only be achieved through formal instruction and through contrastive analysis of language varieties by teaching students to identify and explore differences through classroom activities (Delpit, 1988; Fogel & Ehri, 2000; Pandey, 2000; Rickford, 2006; Rickford & Rickford, 1995; Wolfram et al., 1999). Rickford argues that that the contrastive analysis approach uses student fluency in their first language variety as a 'springboard' for developing fluency in the prestige variety valued by schools; in this way, it 'proceeds from a position of strength' (Rickford, 2006: 83). Rickford (2006) also argues that this approach allows teachers to systematically target problem areas for students, thus allowing for increased efficiency in the classroom. Rickford (2006) offers two final arguments in support of the contrastive analysis approach (a) that ad hoc methods of ignoring or, conversely, constantly correcting minority language varieties does not seem to work and (b) there are several empirical studies that support the effectiveness of using contrastive analysis. Rickford's arguments demonstrate the importance of considering the relationship between fluency in the language variety used for formal reading instruction.

Educational researchers have also explored the implications of linguistic bias in assessment tools designed to measure students' oral and written language skills (Godley et al., 2007; Patton, 2008). Speech and language pathologists, resource room teachers, psychologists and special educators generally perform these assessments by using standardized tests. While the creators of such tests have certainly attempted to address concerns related to problems of culturally biased norming, Long and Christensen (1998) argue that no standardized test can ever be completely unbiased, making the use of such tests questionable in the high-stakes situation of directing the educational path of any student, but particularly those who do not belong to the majority language groups upon which these tests are normed. In spite of such warnings regarding standardized tests that have not been appropriately normed or modified for use with a local population, such instruments continue to be used when assessing minority populations (Long & Christensen, 1998). Biased assessment can result in misdiagnosis of speech, language and learning difficulties, which, in turn, can potentially further exacerbate students' attempts to develop literacy skills in mainstream classrooms (Harris, 1985).

The above-described areas of research are some key areas of exploration in English language variation and schools. Others include the relationships between identity (teacher and student), power and English language variation (Delpit, 1988, 2006; Delpit & Kilgour Dowdy, 2002); influencing teacher linguistic bias by introducing 'linguistic knowledge' or 'dialect awareness' (Abdul-Hakim, 2002; Blake & Cutler, 2003; Bündgens-Kosten, 2009; Patton, 2008); cultural conceptualizations and considerations in non-school-sanctioned English varieties (Lee, 2006; Malcolm & Sharifian, 2002; Sharifian, 2001, 2006; Sharifian et al., 2004) and the place and value of 'nonstandard' English language varieties in the classroom (Blake & Van Sickle, 2001; Sharifian, 2008; Siegel 2006, 2007). A number of monographs, edited volumes and journal articles provide excellent research-based entry points into the ideas I have described in this section, as well as other studies not mentioned here. For example, a 2006 volume edited by Shondel Nero provides readers with a broad range of papers conducted around English language varieties and creoles in schools. It is also worth noting that Nero (2006a) includes explorations of many English language varieties and creoles (e.g. beyond simply African American English) including Caribbean, Hawai'ian, African and Asian Englishes. A recent monograph by John Edwards (2010) groups English language variation with second and foreign language education under the umbrella term 'language diversity' and explores the pedagogical implications of linguistically diverse classrooms. Walt Wolfram, Carolyn Temple Adger and Donna Christian's well-known 1999 monograph explores English variation in the United States and provides readers with research-based pedagogical tools and materials. Lisa Delpit and Joanne Kilgour Dowdy's edited volume (2002) includes previously published papers as well as original work, many written from a first-person perspective, exploring the relationships between language, identity and power. Finally, those readers interested in a condensed overview of recent research in English language variation, creoles and schools could turn to Jeff Siegel's 2007 journal-length paper.

The review I provided in this section is not meant to be exhaustive but seeks, rather, to provide the reader with a general sense of the ways in which research has approached the study of English language variation in educational settings over the past approximately 40 years. The research methods employed are diverse as are the aspects of English language variation explored. There are, however, some common threads in this research that I would like to highlight. First, it would be safe to say that all authors are in agreement that there is much to be done in improving the educational experiences of students who speak English language varieties not sanctioned by schools. That is, the existence of linguistic imbalances is a common assumption of all the research reviewed in this section. Second, there also seems to be an underlying belief among many, but not all, that once the 'best practice' or missing information (i.e. a particular pedagogical intervention or dialect awareness training) is discovered that well-intentioned educators will experience what Bündgens-Kosten (2009) refers to as a 'linguistic epiphany', that is, that educators will realize the error of their linguistically biased ways and choose to right any linguistic wrongs of which they were previously unaware. This is a key point of departure for my work and for the analysis and arguments of this book. While I do believe that linguistic information and pedagogical innovations are necessary, I put forward the idea that there is another step involved in the process of dismantling linguistic bias in settler schools.

I want to suggest that English language variation research conducted in societies founded on racial hierarchies (in places such as Canada, the United States, Australia and New Zealand) could benefit from considering the continuing historical and societal influences of colonialism and nationalism on the racialized identities of teachers and students and school language and literacy practices. It is significant that teaching populations in settler societies consist of predominantly white bodies viewed as speakers of 'Standard English'. These teachers continue to be constructed by colonial and national ideologies that position them as the unmarked linguistic and racial norm.

Positioned in this way, the likely outcome for white settler teachers who have not yet developed critical awareness is to view other Englishes as deviations from the norm and to treat them, and their speakers, as something that needs correction and remediation. This reality and the pedagogical outcomes it produces should not be ignored in the analysis of English language variation. Such a reality calls for an overtly political and critical direction in English language variation research in settler societies.

A Critical Direction for English Language Variation and Education

This section introduces the critical framework that informs the writing of this book. As I have mentioned before, I draw on writings typically described as critical race and postcolonial theory. My reasons for doing so are two-fold. First, as I have already mentioned, I add this layer because I believe that it is necessary to re-educate ourselves about our colonial pasts and present if we want make changes in present-day educational inequity. These particular historical events continue to construct identities, privilege and inequity in settler societies; educator linguistic bias in settler societies is but one of the many consequences of colonialism and nationalism. Continuing to deal with the surface problems I described in the previous section is a bit like having a leaky basement and solving the problem by mopping the floor when it rains instead of repairing the crack in the foundation. No matter which mop you buy or who does the mopping, the crack is going to stay where it is and continue to allow rain into your basement.

While treating educator linguistic bias as a lack of information about how languages function or searching for the best type of pedagogical intervention may be part of the process towards creating equitable education (just as mopping up the floor is part of cleaning up after a flood), these views of educator linguistic bias may fail to recognize its origins; its role in a larger system and its purpose. Educator linguistic bias in settler schools contributes to the production and maintenance of the past and present-day racial, ethnic and linguistic hierarchies of societies European imperialism created throughout the world. Viewing educator linguistic bias as a colonial practice, tool and encounter is an essential step towards change.

Second, my choice is to create this critical framework by drawing on ideas from postcolonial theory and CRT in writing this book is also motivated by a desire to see more critical thinking in the academic community of which I am member: applied linguistics. Alastair Pennycook (2001) argues for the need to develop historical understanding in applied linguistics and describes 'postcolonial perspectives' as being useful for thinking about language and diversity. Too often, educational discussions of language variation are disconnected from the larger social and historical context in which they occur. Pennycook explains that '[it] is common to view applied linguistics as concerned with language in context, but the conceptualization is frequently one that is limited to an overlocalized and undertheorized view of social relations' (Pennycook, 2001: 5). This more common view of applied linguistics allows for the mapping of micro-relations but excludes the mapping of macro-relations such as the relationships between language variation and colonialism. Any discussions, such as those in this book, that delve into issues such as educational inequity, linguistic prescriptivism, race, settler-indigenous relations and biased pedagogy need to be firmly grounded in the historical, social and political events that created these societal institutions, racialized beings, inequity and privilege.

Theoretical Contributions from Postcolonial Thinking

As a method of academic inquiry, postcolonial theory has been used to examine and critique power relations in a range of contexts and ways. Some broad topics include: the formation of empire; the impact of colonization on postcolonial history, economy, science and culture; the cultural productions of colonized societies; and agency for colonized peoples. As an academic discipline, postcolonial theory seeks to answer questions such as: How did colonialism happen? How did the experience of colonization affect those who were colonized as well as the colonizers? What are the continuing aftereffects of colonial education, science and technology in postcolonial societies? What were the forms of resistance against colonial control? How do gender, race and class function in colonial and postcolonial discourse? Are new forms of imperialism replacing colonization and how?

Postcolonial critiques and the terminology they use including *Self, Other, Inner Circle, Centre, Periphery, Othering* and *Alterity* are influenced by critiques of Western philosophical ideas. In order to understand postcolonial thinking and the above-mentioned terms, then, it is necessary to know a little bit about Western philosophy and the kinds of debates that have occurred between philosophers in the past four centuries. As such, a brief overview of European philosophy – specifically Cartesian philosophy and the ideas and thinking that derive from it – is necessary because this particular view of the world underlies European colonial movements and thinking (past and present). This summary is mine, but it should be noted that this section is largely informed by Leela Gandhi's (1998) examination of the history of postcolonial theory and by the theorizing of Indigenous scholars who oppose Western cognitive imperialism (Atleo, 2004; Battiste, 2000; Cajete, 2000; Kawagley, 1995; Little Bear, 2000; Smith, 2000). Any readers with an interest in a more thorough understanding of the origins of the reasoning that helped to make colonialism possible or in alternatives to western philosophy could look to these sources as starting points.

French poststructuralist theorists like Derrida and Foucault and other earlier philosophers like Heidegger, Adorno and Nietzsche have all theorized about the influence of Cartesian philosophy, a particular Western worldview first unleashed in 1619 by French philosopher René Descartes. Working under a humanistic assumption – the idea that despite our many differences, the human experience has a universal and given nature – Descartes was trying to make sense of the world by determining what things all human beings know for certain. To this end, Descartes posited that there is nothing that humans can be certain of other than the *Self*: the individual person's own existence in the world. From this idea comes the familiar statement (known as Descartes' cogito) 'I think therefore I am,' which is central to Cartesian philosophy and probably familiar to most readers. These words might seem harmless but it is the thinking born out of this seemingly innocuous statement that laid the groundwork for much of European philosophy that would follow the time of Descartes and for movements such as European colonialism and fascism (Gandhi, 1998).

Cartesian philosophy placed European humans at the centre of their worlds and allowed them (and, subsequently, many others) to believe that nature could be controlled through acquisition of knowledge and classification and analysis of the surrounding world. The experiences of other humans different from the Self – commonly referred to as the *Other* – and other types of life such as plants and animals are not part of this philosophy's view of the world except in how they are viewed or understood by the Self. Cartesian philosophy omits the Other and focuses solely on the Self and the Self's view, definition and classification of the surrounding world. This way of thinking about the world links power to the individual's ability to define the world; anything that eludes or defies classification is, therefore, troublesome. In an effort to make sense of the world and to maintain power though knowing, Cartesian man must either omit or suppress the deviant ways of the other. With Cartesian philosophy in mind, we can start to understand the 'civilizing' goals of colonialism; colonialist and nationalist education; and educator linguist bias as the fear and suppression of *alterity* (the state of being other) through the pursuit of sameness.

Cartesian philosophy went on to inform most of European philosophy in the 17th and 18th centuries, including the Age of Enlightenment, a time in European philosophy which saw *reason* as the primary source of authority. The Enlightenment is also influential in making possible the type of thinking known as *modernity*. Canagarajah reminds us that enlightenment, rationalism, science and modernism had radical beginnings: 'they championed the thinking, observation, and experience of the individual against the dogmas of the state, aristocracy, and Church' (Canagarajah, 1999: 17). As radical as these processes might have initially been, modernist notions subsequently allowed Europeans to believe it possible for humankind to move from immaturity to maturity (i.e. develop) through the search for knowledge as a means to controlling nature. This idea created the sense that European rationality allows for the possibility of improvement for all of humanity.

Modern philosophy as I describe it in this chapter continues to influence our present-day realities. Ashcroft explains that 'the Cartesian separation of subject and object, the separation of the consciousness from the world of which it is conscious, is the schema which still underlies the modern Western episteme with its passion for "scientific" objectivity and its tendency to see the world as a continuum of technological data' (Ashcroft, 2001: 67). This view of the world also leads to the suppression of non-Western knowledge systems (Atleo, 2004; Battiste, 2000; Cajete, 2000; Kawagley, 1995; Little Bear, 2000; Smith, 2000). Cartesian philosophy inevitably produced ways of viewing the world that positioned the white European (and, subsequently, settler) Self as the centre of the world gazing outwardly; as ignorant or scared of the Other; and as understanding the Self as having an ethical responsibility to bring the European rationality to others, so that they too could progress from immaturity to maturity. If you will permit me to momentarily skip forward to other chapters in this book, I would like to point out that this view of the world, first put forth in 1619, sounds eerily similar to many present-day settler school approaches to 'educating' Indigenous students.

Postcolonial thinking provides approaches to thinking about colonial constructs such as *standard languages* and *dialects*. Highlighting the significant role of colonialism by including historical accounts in analyses is one approach that will be employed in subsequent chapters of this book. Spivak (1990, 1999) tells us that colonialism cannot be relegated to the past because it continues to construct the present, an argument echoed by Pennycook in his calls for greater focus on macro-relations in applied linguistics research (2001). Leela Gandhi explains that independence from direct colonial rule is often accompanied by a desire 'to forget the colonial past' (Leela Gandhi, 1998: 4). Razack argues that amnesia about the past in white settler societies 'allows white subjects to be produced as innocent, entitled, rational, and legitimate' (Razack, 2002: 19).

Statements like 'I wasn't there' or 'get over it, the past is the past' in reference to events like the white settler enslavement of Africans for work in the plantations of the United States or the trauma of missionary, boarding and residential schools for Indigenous students in Australia, the United States and Canada, respectively, are some small examples of discourses influenced by a desire to forget the colonial past. Treating educator linguistic bias as a lack of linguistic information is another instance of forgetfulness about the colonial past and, thus, continues the process of constructing white settler subjects as 'innocent'. With these ideas in mind, I argue that working towards improving language bias and educational inequity in settler schools must involve the work of remembering our colonial pasts and developing an understanding that colonialism continues to produce our present, including racialized identities; societal (and educator) views about language; and linguistic dominance and oppression.

How else might postcolonial thinking inform educational research in English language variation? Andreotti (2007) provides a synthesis of potential connections that can be made between the writing of postcolonial theorist Gayatri Spivak and education. While Spivak addresses education in relation to 'North–South' encounters, her ideas can also be adapted for this book's analysis of settler school educator linguistic bias, particularly in terms of the steps involved in 'establishing an ethical relation to the Other', a consideration that I argue is missing from how we have typically examined language variation in schools. Spivak's four steps for educators working towards establishing this 'ethical relation to the Other', as outlined in Andreotti (2007), might be summarized in the following way: (a) educators must engage in the sustained critique of dominant discourses (i.e. deconstruction); (b) educators must become 'hyper self-reflexive' and develop awareness of their own complicities; (c) educators must 'unlearn their privilege' and be prepared to de-centre knowledge; and (d) educators must be prepared to 'work without guarantees'. Were we to apply these steps to the study of English language variation and educator linguistic bias, educators and teacher educators might work towards: developing their own critical awareness of standard language ideologies; learning to understand and acknowledge how standard language ideologies benefit us as white settler educators; changing practices in classrooms that privilege speakers of settler English varieties; and also understanding that there is no 'best practice' that is going to guarantee success. As this book will show, the evidence of such thinking in the school where I conducted my research is limited.

Instead, settler educators seem stuck in the centuries-old pattern of noticing the alterity or 'lack' of First Nations and Métis students' language. Consider for example, an excerpt from an interview with Lisa, a white settler educator in my study:

> I'm all for the full time kindergarten for the children that need it, not everybody but those kids that aren't getting enough language, so starting sooner.

Lisa attributes her First Nations and Métis students' language 'deficits', a term she uses throughout our interview, to a lack of exposure to language in their homes. In her statement, we can see the colonial discourse of noticing alterity as well as that of positioning the self as the bringer of rationality, progress and development through exposure to schools at earlier age, so that First Nations and Métis students can get 'enough language'.

In summary, the postcolonial lens that I have described in this section includes: a historical view of educator linguistic bias; an awareness of the self and other construct; an awareness of the fear and suppression of difference through the promotion of (linguistic) homogeneity; an understanding of the need for deconstructing dominant colonial linguistic discourses; and acknowledgement of the complicity of educators in the ongoing production of colonialism. I want to suggest that these notions must be considered in the analysis of English language variation in a settler school, particularly one in which Indigenous and settler encounters figure so significantly. Combined with the work of ideas coming out of the body of literature known as CRT (to be discussed in the next section of this chapter), these key concepts inform the analyses and findings discussed in subsequent chapters of this book.

Theoretical Contributions from CRT

The previous section highlighted potential contributions of postcolonial theory to this book's analysis of English language variation. Here, I wish to provide an overview of the academic body of writings known as CRT and also outline some of the key concepts of this literature. Rogers Cherland and Harper describe the potential of CRT for thinking about society in the following ways:

> Race is an idea, a discourse, a system, a way of thinking that advantages some people and disadvantages others, a construction that serves certain powerful political and economic interests. Race is socially constructed

but critical race theory points out that race has profound consequences for material well-being in daily life. In a racist society it is difficult to speak openly about race, because social norms are constructed to serve the interests of the status quo, and taboos that silence explicit talk about race serve to maintain the naturalness of White supremacy, and to support the notion that poor people suffer because of their own deficiencies. Critical race theory makes race visible and demonstrates the ways in which the law and educational research (and all other social institutions in a racist society) have been influenced by a paradigmatic view that characterizes people of color as inferior. (Cherland & Harper, 2007: 109)

The fields of postcolonial theory and CRT, as I use them in this book, should be seen as existing in conversation together. Because while academics typically associated with these two theoretical camps may not be speaking to one another (in a literal sense) there is overlap between ideas put forth by the two. Both areas would be aligned in acknowledging: settler society as a historically constructed racial hierarchy; the importance of practicing reflexivity and developing critical literacy (or participating in deconstruction); and race as a social construct. They also differ in a number of ways, which will become obvious through the discussions in this section. The most salient difference, perhaps, is that CRT can be described as more action oriented than postcolonial theory. While postcolonial theory provides a lens for the critique of education in settler societies, CRT says 'adopting and adapting CRT as a framework for educational equity means that we will have to expose racism in education *and* propose radical solutions for addressing it' (Ladson-Billings, 1998: 27, emphasis in the original text). As such, CRT contributes to this study in ways that postcolonial theory cannot. These differences make it necessary to provide an overview of CRT as it relates to the study of education.

CRT first emerged as a form of legal critique in the mid-1970s in the United States with the writings of Derrick Bell and Alan Freeman (Delgado, 1995). Both were dissatisfied with the slow pace around racial reform and traditional civil rights strategies. Four main tenets of CRT are described as typifying this field of studies. CRT (a) names racism as normal and starts from the common assumption that American society is racist, privileges whites and marginalizes peoples of colour; (b) uses stories to allow the sharing of lived experiences of peoples of colour; (c) challenges the liberal notion that social reform is possible without radical change; and (d) questions the value of civil rights legislation in the United States, arguing that it has done more to privilege whites than it has to reduce the effects of racism on peoples of colour (Crosland Nebeker, 1998; Delgado, 1995; Ladson-Billings, 1998). The American origins of CRT are obvious; this body of literature tends to focus on the United States and on the experiences of African Americans. Having said this, the key ideas of CRT can be adopted and employed in the Canadian context (and other societies too).

In the study of education, CRT has been gaining in visibility and influence for roughly 15 years since first being introduced in the form of an article written by Gloria Ladson-Billings and William Tate (Dixon & Rousseau, 2005; Ladson-Billings & Tate, 1994). While CRT has its roots in legal studies, there are a number of ways that it can be useful in the study of schools. Ladson-Billings explains that it is 'because of the meaning and value imputed to whiteness that CRT becomes an important intellectual and social tool for deconstruction, reconstruction, and construction: deconstruction of oppressive structures and discourses, reconstruction of human agency, and construction of equitable and socially just relations of power' (Ladson-Billings, 1998: 9). As an analytical approach, then, CRT provides ways of 'noticing' whiteness. To be more specific, from a critical race perspective, a school curriculum is viewed as a 'culturally specific artifact designed to maintain a White supremacist master script' (Ladson-Billings, 1998: 18). Similarly, CRT maintains that present-day pedagogy begins from the starting point of viewing minority students as deficient. Ladson-Billings explains (with a focus on African American students) that 'as a consequence, classroom teachers are engaged in a never-ending quest for "the right strategy or technique" to deal with (read: control) "at-risk" (read: African American) students. Cast in a language of failure, instructional approaches for African American students typically involve some aspect of remediation' (Ladson-Billings, 1998: 19). Finally, viewed through the lens of critical theory, standardized intelligence testing is nothing more than an organized attempt to 'legitimize African American deficiency under the guise of scientific rationalism' (Ladson-Billings, 1998: 19).

CRT informs the writing of this book in several significant ways. First, I attempt to name racism and speak openly about whiteness, race and white supremacy in the ways modelled by writers such as Gloria Ladson-Billings and Adrienne Dixon. Second, CRT acknowledges the experiential knowledge of people of colour. Matsuda explains that 'those who have experienced discrimination speak with a special voice to which we should listen' (Matsuda, 1995: 63). Accordingly, I foreground the words of First Nations educators (Deborah, in particular) in my study when they name racist practices in this particular settler school. CRT is also helpful as an analytical tool when issues of colour-blindness and 'denial of difference' (Dei, 1999: 17) emerge in the educator interview data. As white settlers in a white settler society, many of us are particularly adept at talking about race without talking about race as well as denying its relevance to Canadian society. For this study, then, CRT provides the vocabulary necessary for talking about colour-blindness as a phenomenon. Let me provide an example from my classroom research.

I hit brick walls with some interviewees in my research as soon as I described students as *white* or *First Nations*. Conducting my interview with Karen, a white settler educator, was when I first came to the realization that colour blindness needed to be considered in this book. Karen was unwilling to discuss students in terms of race because she explained that she did not think of them 'like that'. Her reticence to discuss her students in terms of racial group membership forced me to discard the majority of my questions. In our interview, I initially tried to navigate around her avoidance of race as can be seen in the following exchange:

Andrea: And do any of the children see speech and language specialists?
Karen: I've got one, two, three, four
Andrea: Uh-huh, okay, and of your group, you said 18, did you tell me? Um, and I know you maybe don't think about them this way, but just for the purpose of my interview, would you be able to tell me how many have an Indigenous background?
Karen: No, I can't but I can get my register

Karen was surprised when I took her up on her offer but did retrieve her class register and was able to rapidly scan the list and give me the names of her First Nations and Métis students who see speech and language specialists. Her ability to quickly provide me with the answer to my question indicates to me that she does, indeed, know which children are First Nations or Métis and which children are white settlers in spite of her initial claims of colour-blindness.

Karen was not the only teacher to deny awareness of race. Some were uncomfortable with my use of the term *white*, preferring to use *non-Native*. One First Nations educator named Nicole also stated to me that she was 'beyond race' and another First Nations educator explained to me that 'kids are just kids.' These colour-blind statements should not be all that surprising given that, as Dixson and Rousseau state, 'the dominant discourse positions colour-blindness as an ideal' (Dixson & Rousseau, 2005: 14). These educators' reactions to my question also bring to mind Schick and St Denis's descriptions of the ideological assumptions commonly held by white settler teachers-in-training in Saskatchewan. Certainly, Karen's behaviour provides evidence of assuming the positions that '(1) race does not matter; (2) everyone has equal opportunity; and (3) through individual acts and good intentions one can secure innocence as well as superiority' (Schick & St Denis, 2003: 1). Yet, as CRT maintains, the reality is that race does matter, not everyone has the same opportunities and we are all complicit within the colonialist systems that operate in settler societies. Innocence is not possible.

Furthermore, we can also examine the assumption that it is somehow offensive to 'notice' someone's race. In fact, to whitewash all students should likely be seen as a more damaging alternative. Take, for example, the findings of Rousseau and Tate (2003), a study of high-school mathematics teachers. In this study, teachers were unwilling, much like Karen, to acknowledge patterns in achievement along race lines or to talk about the role possibly played by racism in influencing the academic performances of students of colour. These teachers avoided race as a topic of discussion in two ways: (1) they simply denied that race played a role in any differences of achievement (similar to Karen's approach) or (2) they attributed differences to socio-economic status rather than institutional racism. The second way of excluding race as a topic of conversation was also used by participants in my study. The following exchange with Corrine, a white settler educator, shows evidence of this pattern:

Andrea: Do you have any feelings about literacy development in grade 1, grade 2, why there is this discrepancy between First Nations and white children?
Corrine: A lot of the problem in this area is poverty and poverty is a huge issue, and I think that has so much more bearing on the gap between reading

Rousseau and Tate maintain that educator colour-blindness actually prevented the mathematics teachers involved in their study from reflecting upon their own complicity in the production of the underachievement of their students of colour. It is possible that colour-blindness plays a similar role for educator participants in my study.

Finally, I also want to touch on another argument from CRT that contributes to this study's theoretical framework: the notion of 'race, within the scheme of whiteness [...] as a malady' (Dixon & Rousseau, 2005: 16). This position maintains only if we view whiteness as 'normal' that any person who is not white has to been seen as abnormal. Dixon and Rousseau explain:

Thus, within polite, middle class mores, it is impolite to see when someone is *different*, abnormal, and thus, *not white*. Hence it is better to ignore, or become colour-blind, than to notice that people of colour have the physical malady of skin colour, or *not whiteness*. Similarly, Thompson (1998) points out that 'politely pretending not to notice students' color makes no sense unless being of different colors is somehow shameful' (p. 524). When students begin to internalize this shame or sense of abnormality, colour-blindness can become a form of microagression. (Dixon & Rousseau, 2005: 16, emphasis in the original)

As Cherland and Harper maintain, 'taboos that silence explicit talk about race serve to maintain the naturalness of White supremacy' (Cherland & Harper, 2007: 109). As a teacher, it is impossible to reconcile the racial inequity of Canadian schools with colour-blind and multicultural discourses that circulate in Canadian educational communities. Too often, the present-day strategy to explaining this reality continues to be a deficit approach that places blame on family and home. CRT recognizes the racial bias in present-day educational practices and provides the epistemological foundation that permits this book to name racism as a component of educator linguistic bias in settler schools.

Conclusion

The theoretical framework that informs this book derives from two theoretical fields that contribute in different ways: (1) postcolonial theory helps us to understand the continuing relevancy of colonialism in terms of economic oppression and exploitation and as a form of cognitive imperialism that leads to societal hierarchies as well as racial and linguistic inequity and (2) CRT points out that race and racism can never be viewed as irrelevant in settler societies (born as they are out of conquest and invasion). These bodies of writing can help in terms of understanding why some languages are legitimate and others are not; what we do as humans in settler society to produce this situation; as well as how it affects the lives of those who live within this society.

From this theoretical framework, if you are not a speaker of a legitimate language variety, you lack the linguistic capital to gain access to education, employment and housing. This reality is not a 'given', but results from a society born out of British imperialism and settler colonialism. This critical approach is useful in learning to see schools as white spaces and provides insight into how the racialization of space and of bodies occurs. It allows us to see the positioning of particular language varieties as illegitimate as a cog in the wheel that produces whiteness. Each of these fields helps to extend this book's analysis beyond observations of Deborah's classroom.

The types of research described in the first section of this chapter tend to be more localized in their focus. I would also suggest that there is a tendency to focus on language in isolation from society and in an ahistorical manner. Had I followed some of the more prevalent trends in the study of English language variation, I might have chosen to present a linguistic description of the English spoken by students in Deborah's classroom or perhaps focused on the attitudes of individual teachers in the school. Instead, this book's discussion is not limited to an analysis of what occurs inside the school walls or during the 2005–2006 school year. My exploration of educator linguistic bias includes historical overviews and discussions of colonialism; a sustained focus on racialized identity; and an understanding of schools as white spaces that participate in the production and maintenance of racial hierarchies through language and literacy instruction, among other pedagogical practices.

The chapters that follow shift in and out of the past, present, local and global and focus on revealing the racialization of educational agents; school spaces; English language varieties; and educator linguistic bias. I suggest that this multifaceted analysis is necessary in order to produce a more complete and complicated view of educator linguistic bias in settler schools. For example, talking about cities as racialized spaces and schools as sites of whiteness, as I do in Chapter 5, is part of deconstructing why some English language varieties are allowed in these spaces and others are not. Similarly, the work of unpacking the 'how' and 'why' of educators' views of the Englishes of children like Crystal, Amber and James begins with the description of the racialized history and construction of the place these educational agents inhabit in Chapter 3. These steps are necessary in order to understand 'proper English' as the colonial construct that it is.

3 Colonial Ideologies and Discourses

Introduction

My undergraduate education students often arrive at their first language and literacies education courses with me with an understanding of the past as the past. I work towards moving beyond this thinking early on in our time together for a number of reasons, one of which includes my thoughts around the influence of history on our beliefs about what constitutes legitimate language. Developing a historically situated understanding of educator linguistic bias is necessary for destabilizing normative views of language. As I suggest throughout this book, the past continues to influence the present in ways we often do not understand. But how does this exactly happen? What kinds of mechanisms allow historical events and movements of 500 years ago to continue influencing our present? Why is the past not just the past?

In the previous chapters, I introduced the idea that present-day views of language are linked to larger societal processes such as imperialism and colonialism as well the types of discourses that accompany these systems. Before moving to a discussion of some of the intricacies and functions of these systems, let me take a moment to clarify my use of some key terms linked to these processes: empire, imperialism and colonialism. An *empire* can be thought of as 'a relationship of domination and subordination between one polity (called the *metropole*) and one or more territories (called colonies) that lie outside the metropole's boundaries yet are claimed as its lawful possessions' (Abernethy, 2000: 19). England, France and Spain are all former metropoles that ruled vast territories. The process of how empires get built and the implications of this process lead to two significant terms used in this chapter: *imperialism* and *colonialism*. Sometimes, *imperialism* and *colonialism* seem to be used interchangeably. The two terms are closely related, but they do represent different processes. *Imperialism* can be thought of as the process of constructing an empire that leads to domination and control of colonies. *Colonialism* represents the policies, practices and ideologies used by a metropole (or settlers within the colony) to retain control of a colony and to benefit from that control. These terms, and the constructs they represent, are explored throughout this chapter.

It is not possible to understand classroom interaction and educational inequity without examining the historical and social processes of the settler society in which the school and school agents are located. Educator views of language must be seen in connection with larger societal processes such as imperialism, colonialism and nationalism and the discourses that accompany these systems. The purpose of this chapter, then, is to (a) develop an understanding of the ways in which ideologies and discourses function within societies and (b) provide a historical overview of European imperialist movements; colonial discourses and the nature and goals of colonialism and nationalism in settler societies.

Ideologies and Discourses

The notions of *ideology* and *discourse* are useful for understanding how normative views of human behaviour, and language in particular, get produced and reproduced. In applied linguistics, the term *discourse* has been used to describe both an 'instance of language use' (Pennycook, 1994: 115) as well as something larger that influences 'why and how a person comes to say certain things' (Pennycook, 1994: 119). Pennycook describes the difference between these two meanings of *discourse* in the following way 'there is a position that emphasizes language as a system and then looks to discourse analysis to explain how various contextual factors affect language in use, and, on the other, there is a position that looks at how meanings are a product of social and cultural relationships and then turns to see how these may be realized in language' (Pennycook, 1994: 115). I am interested in this second use of the term as well as its relationship with *ideology*.

Ideology and *discourse* are useful because they help us to see the underlying societal structures that play a role in producing educational inequity and the systems in which we are all implicated. As academic terms, *discourse* and *ideology* are defined and used in different ways by a number of scholarly thinkers (Bourdieu, Fairclough, Foucault, Gee, Pennycook and Canagarajah, to name only a few). Foucault, for example, uses *discourse* in three ways: all documents, texts and utterances that have meaning and affect the world; as groups of utterances that appear to be regulated in some way; and as a regulated practice or rules and structures that serve to produce certain types of utterances, documents, and texts. These descriptions of *discourse* tend to have blurred boundaries and, in many cases, overlap with one another. For Fairclough, *discourse* is 'language as social practice', a definition that

Pennycook sees as having connections to both uses of *discourse* in applied linguistics (Fairclough, 1994: 121). Pennycook suggests that Fairclough's use of the terms includes both 'chunks of language as its actually used' but also 'relates language to other social practices' and sees language practice as 'socially determined' (Fairclough, 1994: 121). Fairclough sees language use as a social act in itself. 'Such acts, furthermore, are not individualistic acts of language users in cognitive isolation, but rather are determined by the larger social and ideological conditions of society' (Pennycook, 1994: 121).

There are several differences between Fairclough's and Foucault's writings on discourse (Pennycook, 1994). The one I would like to focus on here is their views on the relationship between ideology and discourse. Fairclough views ideology as that which determines discourse. Foucault's view is that there are no undetermined states that exist outside of discourse; there are only other discourses shaping the subject. Like Fairclough, however, others see the concepts of ideology and discourse as related, as suggested by Canagarajah's description of discourse as 'the linguistic realization of the social construct ideology' (Canagarajah, 1999: 30). From this view, ideologies are our socially constructed views of the world which, in turn, produce discourses that 'are linguistically manifested in texts' (Canagarajah, 1999: 30). This view of the relationship between ideologies and discourses, as discussed by both Fairclough and Canagarajah, informs the arguments of this chapter.

In discussions of discourses, the use of *text* is broad and can include items such as: books, movies, speeches, advertisements, graffiti, court transcripts, school curriculum, magazine columns and radio and television shows. Discourses, or sets of statements that are viewed as 'normal' or 'commonplace' about the state of world and humans' place and behaviour, circulate within these texts. These discourses, then, regulate the actions and practices of humans and institutions. Though determining how societal discourses regulate social identities and relationships may seem abstract, it does have some practical implications. For example, once you determine (e.g. through discourse analysis) that a particular ideology is determining discourses that are circulated through photographs in magazine advertisements or images in children's textbooks, the potential exists to counter such discourses by introducing alternatives. Similarly, critical literacy skills, or the ability to recognize biased discourses, provide human subjects with the ability to choose or introduce alternative discourses. Understanding and recognizing the function of discourses and the ways in which we are regulated by them are important tools in dismantling colonialist systems that continue to operate in present-day settler societies.

Ideologies, and the discourses they produce, can have long shelf lives. My colleague Valerie Mulholland describes colonial discourses, in particular, as having the atomic half-life of a cheese slice. This longevity is because discourses (and what they exclude) become normalized so that we make assumptions about what is normal and what is not based on the types of messages we see circulating in societal texts and, subsequently, behave accordingly. Because of their seemingly common sense or natural nature, repressive or harmful ideologies need to be systematically worked at through a combination of critically reading existing discourses and through the introduction of alternative discourses (e.g. through movements like feminism). Left unchecked, discourses simply continue to operate as 'natural' or 'common sense' or morph into new versions (which continue to sustain dominant discourses) since they derive from the same pre-existing ideologies. Worked at from the other direction, through the introduction of alternative discourses, there is the potential to change ideologies. This possibility is good news for educators and teacher educators.

Imperialism and colonialism are not simply periods of time or histories of conquest. Ideologies and discourses accompanied these processes and the passing of time does not automatically imply that colonial discourses ceased to circulate within the societies produced by these movements. When we speak of decolonizing a society, it is the resiliency of colonial and settler ideologies and discourses that make decolonization difficult. Dismantling systems and practices that make colonial constructs such as residential schools and reserve pass systems possible is necessary but without an awareness of ideologies and discourses, the danger is that new colonial practices emerge in their place. Learning to deconstruct colonial discourses about identities, nations, languages and literacy is a necessary step in moving towards equitable practices in schools. Having discussed the relationship between ideologies and discourses, I move now to examining some of the ideologies that accompanied European imperialism and settler colonialism in Canada. Understanding the types of thinking and messages of these movements will help us to recognize similar patterns in our thinking around English language varieties.

European Expansion and Settler Colonialism

The chronicle of imperialist expansions that I present here examines the aspirations and movements of European colonies over the last five centuries. This overview is necessary so that the presence of colonial languages in countries such as Brazil, Mexico, Haiti and Canada can be contextualized and understood as 'fully colonial' (Razack, 2002) and not simply as something that happened by accident, amicably, or without agents. Academic writing about world languages sometimes ignores or minimizes imperialist history in discussions about the 'spread' of languages spoken extensively throughout the world. For example, David Crystal's 1995 *Cambridge Encyclopedia of the English Language* describes the arrival of English-speaking colonists to the United States, Canada, Australia, New Zealand, South Africa, South Asia, Colonial Africa, South-East Asia and the South Pacific in what might be interpreted as neutral terms. His is an exhaustive and well-researched piece of material; yet little is mentioned of the range of Indigenous languages that were already spoken in these places nor the violence, invasion and assimilatory projects that accompanied English in its movement around the globe. Omissions of this nature in historical publications such as encyclopedias and textbooks that are used in schools are part of the process through which the self and other are constructed. I see the postcolonial examination of modern European imperialism in this section as a necessary step in acknowledging the central and enduring role of empire- building in the present-day linguistic realities of colonized nations and settler and Indigenous peoples around the world.

The following facts provide an understanding of just how pervasive and far-reaching European imperialism has been in the five-century span over which it occurred. By the 1930s colonies and ex-colonies covered 84.6% of the land surface of the globe (Loomba, 1998). This figure is shocking in itself but next consider this reality: the eight countries that created these European empires – Portugal, Spain, France, the United Kingdom, the Netherlands, Belgium, Germany and Italy – account for merely 1.6% of the land surface of the earth. Finally, in addition to territorial expansion, we also see European expansion reflected in the following fact: 'an estimated 700 million people living outside Europe speak English, French, Portuguese, or Spanish in the home' (Abernethy, 2000: 15). European countries claimed vast territories as their own and, in doing so, asserted their rights to rule over hundreds of millions of humans; these movements changed the landscape of the world. What kinds of ideologies might have permitted these countries to believe in their rights to extend their claims to land surface and human lives in this manner?

Sunera Thobani explains that European rationalization of these expansions derived from variations of the following beliefs:

> Indigenous peoples were not fully human; they were not Christian, they were not civilized; they had not evolved; they were doomed to extinction by history and progress; they had no recognizable legal systems or concepts of property rights and were thus lawless; and they did not cultivate their land. (Thobani, 2007: 41)

When I first read that excerpt from Thobani (2007), I was struck by how much it reminded me of something a research participant said to me during a 2003 research project in another settler community in Saskatchewan (Sterzuk, 2003). During a conversation over coffee in the staff room, a male white settler teacher and I were talking about my life in Quebec. During the conversation, the man asked me about Indigenous peoples who live in this part of Canada and suggested that they were more developed than 'our natives' because they had 'at least' developed some farming practices prior to the arrival of Europeans. His words were disturbing considering the high numbers of First Nations and Métis students under his tutelage but also fascinating when you consider how they mirror the legal doctrine of *terra nullius* or the idea that land was empty or uninhabited if the people were not Christian or agricultural. This idea, first employed in the 1500s, was used in the rationalization of European expansion. How does an idea like *terra nullius* get introduced in the 1500s in Europe and then surface in a settler school in Saskatchewan in 2002 out of the mouth of an elementary school teacher?

Imperial discourses informed European expansions and the histories of all continents in the world. The violence of each imperial power sustained the larger imperial and colonial processes. Beginning with the Portuguese expansion of the 15th century, European powers were successful, through genocidal violence, in 'destroying or subjugating the self determination of numerous indigenous societies, despite the intense resistance they encountered' (Thobani, 2007: 42). This genocidal violence included the 'rights' of Europeans to kill heathens in the process of conquering, occupying and possessing land. In achieving European expansion, wars were waged, diseases were spread, and starvation, coercion, trickery and deception were employed so as to compel Indigenous peoples 'to negotiate treaties and to gain sexual access to the women' (Thobani, 2007: 42).

In settler societies, European expansion is often explained through discourses such as pioneer myths which regard the seizing of land as somehow necessary due some imagined sparseness of humans, civilization and agriculture. Thobani explains that 'already inhabited nations were simply legally deemed to be uninhabited if the people were not Christian, not agricultural, not commercial, not "sufficiently evolved" or "simply in the way"' (Thobani, 2007: 47). This version of history is Eurocentric in its views and likely inaccurate in terms of its views of pre-contact civilizations. The truth is that, in the Americas and other locations where Europeans invaded and created settlements, there were communities of peoples who had inhabited the lands for tens of thousands of years; had established commerce, and trades; had developed literacies and technologies; and who spoke many languages perfectly suited for their purposes and for any social futures that might have developed with and without European contact.

This brief overview of European imperialism provides a glimpse into just how far-reaching these expansions were. Yet claiming lands was not the extent of Western Europe's dominion-building. Once the process of extending an empire's territory had begun, it was necessary to cement the relationship through a complex series of systems and beliefs that we now refer to as colonialism. As I have mentioned, colonialism refers to the policies, practices and ideologies used by a metropole or settlers within the colony to retain control of a colony and to benefit from that control. Imperial control of colonies took many forms and produced many policies, practices and discourses. While there are similarities to colonial rule in different types of colonies such as colonies of exploitation (e.g. Kenya, Singapore and Nigeria), settler colonies (e.g. Canada, New Zealand and Brazil) and others such as occupation colonies, mixed colonies and plantation colonies, due to this book's focus on settler schools, I will limit this discussion to characteristics and features of colonialism in settler societies.

Colonialism 'deployed diverse strategies and methods of control' in the many locations around the world where European colonies were established and, as such, it is important to avoid monolithic representations of a singular colonial experience (Loomba, 1998: 15). At the same time, these systems 'produced comparable (and somewhat uncannily similar) relations' (Loomba, 1998: 12). Stasiulis and Yuval-Davis explain that similarities between settler societies can be perceived through their shared interests and 'the modelling and borrowing of systems of control over indigenous and migrant populations among settler states. Instances of this were the reserve and pass systems of control over Indigenous peoples, which South African elites borrowed from Canada and Australia, and the "Natal formula" used to restrict the entry of migrant people of colour throughout the British colonies of settlement' (Stasiulis & Yuval-Davis, 1995: 4). Because of these shared interests and similarities in systems, institutions and ideologies of postcolonial nations, ideas deriving from this discussion of a Canadian context might prove useful in analyses of schools in other settler societies due to similarities deriving from these countries' origins as settler colonies. First, Stasiulis and Yuval-Davis explain that, however diverse their origins and development may be, settler colonies share similar features as well as struggles in terms of reconciling heterogeneous societies consisting of Indigenous peoples and settlers (1995). These similarities result from some of the foundational beliefs behind European expansion. Another commonality between diverse settler societies is in the goals of these former colonies to build societies independent of imperial rule. Finally, settler colonies are also united in their need to control Indigenous peoples (Stasiulis & Yuval-Davis, 1995).

Settler colonies can be described as featuring 'extensive systems of exclusion and exploitation of both "indigenous" and "alien" peoples within, exercised through a variety of coercive, ideological, legal, administrative and cooptative mechanisms' (Stasiulis & Yuval-Davis, 1995: 4). Establishment of stable settler rule over colonies occurred in all settler colonies and was 'accompanied by varying levels of physical and cultural genocide, alienation of indigenous land, disruption of indigenous societies, economies and governance, and movements of indigenous resistance' (Stasiulis & Yuval-Davis, 1995: 7). This process consists of two connected and essential factors. First, settlers must maintain control over Indigenous peoples so as to avoid or minimize Indigenous peoples' access to political control or unrest. Second, it is necessary to create a unified settler population which can prove difficult given the diversity in class, ethnicity and religion among settlers. So how are these two facets of creating stable settler rule connected? As difficult as it might be to create a unified settler population, this goal is made possible in settler colonies through settlers' shared need to exert control over Indigenous peoples. Thobani explains that in Canada, as 'divided as they were by class, gender, ethnicity, even by regional and provincial interests, it was most clearly in their common interest in the subjugation of Native peoples that settlers forged a common cause, a cause at the heart of reconstituting themselves as Canadians. Their active participation in, and tacit approval of, the dispossession of Aboriginal peoples enabled various European colonizers and settler to fashion their relationships as nationals with one another, and with their state' (Thobani, 2007: 56). Heterogeneous settler populations could become united in their control over Indigenous peoples.

Because this need to exert control over Indigenous peoples is part of how a diverse settler society reconstitutes itself as Canadian, this need for control does not disappear once land has been seized and occupied. This need, informed by colonial ideologies with the atomic half-life of a cheese slice, manifests in the exertion of control over Indigenous bodies within societal institutions, schools included. Consider, for example, an anecdote shared by Crystal, one of the First Nations children in my study, during one of our interviews. In the passage that follows, Crystal describes her impressions of an incident between Mr Fleury, the school's vice-principal, and herself. Deborah and I also overheard part of this event and witnessed the rest. Let me first situate Crystal's comments with a brief description of what happened. Crystal was working in the hallway with some other students. The school vice-principal walked by and asked Crystal to speak. Instead, she crawled under the table and refused to come out. In response, he reached under the table and grabbed her by the arm and pulled her out. On hearing Crystal's screams, Deborah interceded; took the young girl from the vice-principal's hands; picked her up; and carried her downstairs to the girls' bathroom. As Deborah explained to me afterwards, she also talked to Crystal about avoiding the vice-principal by encouraging her to use the staircase in the building that did not go past his office. In subsequent weeks, I saw her remind Crystal to take this alternate staircase.

I see Deborah's decision to override her administrator's disciplining of Crystal and to protect Crystal by instructing her on how to avoid interaction with the school vice-principal as evidence of Deborah's understanding of the injustice that had occurred; awareness of her First Nations' students vulnerability in the school; and a view of school disciplinary practices as racist. Crystal talked about the incident in an interview with me a few days later. During our discussion, she broached the subject herself during an unrelated conversation about outcomes for children who break rules at her school:

Crystal: Yeah but then, some teachers, they don't follow the rules
Andrea: Hmm, like how do you mean?
Crystal: Like, like, the rules, like hands off and stuff, some teachers just forget the rules
Andrea: Do they forget them with all the kids or just some kids
Crystal: Just some
Andrea: Why do you think it's with those kids?
Crystal: I don't know
Andrea: Does that make you feel mad?
Crystal: Yeah, cause then, cause Mr Fleury he was, he was, he grabbed my cousin Sarah and put her in his office, holding her arm hard
Andrea: And what about you, what did he do to you?
Crystal: Um, when we were over there and when we were talking, he was dragging me and I was holding on to the table and he was pulling me and he made my arms red
Andrea: Yeah, he's not following the rules, right?
Crystal: Hm-hmm
Andrea: Did you tell your mom and dad?
Crystal: No
Andrea: How come?
Crystal: I told Miss Smith (Elaine, the school principal)
Andrea: Yeah
Crystal: And Miss Smith gonna deal with it
Andrea: She is?
Crystal: Yeah

Andrea: Oh, so you told Mrs Smith about that? About how you felt?
Crystal: Hm-hmm
Andrea: Did you talk to Mrs Desjarlais about it?
Crystal: Yep
Andrea: Cause I know Mrs Desjarlais was pretty worried about you
Crystal: I know
Andrea: Cause you know that it's not right that he did that right? You understand that.
Crystal: And Mrs Desjarlais was like 'he can't help it,' and then she, she she, she was like 'let go of her' and then she grabbed me and she came downstairs with me, and the washroom and we were washing our hands off, wash my face and then we came in classroom

The story Crystal shares will likely affect readers in many ways. I find it sad and I am angered by the vice-principal's violent treatment of a young child but I also admire Crystal's resisting of the situation by talking to her principal and viewing the vice-principal's actions as 'rule-breaking'. I think this incident might also be viewed as a story of a child developing an understanding of (a) who she is and her place in the world (one that she is not necessarily going to accept) as well as (b) how some adults respond to her as a result of who she is (and who they are). Matsuda explains that 'those who have experienced discrimination speak with a special voice to which we should listen' (Matsuda, 1995: 63). Deborah's reaction to Crystal's treatment speaks to her immediate understanding of the moment as racially motivated.

Like Deborah, I see the vice-principal's failure to be 'hands-off' as indicative of issues larger than the bad choices of one man on one particular day. Every player's behaviour in this story is fed by centuries-old colonial discourses and patterns that continue to circulate in settler Canada, including within the institution of schools. Deborah's comments to Crystal about the vice-principal not being able to 'help it' speaks to Deborah's embodied understanding of the ingrained colonial patterns of settler control over Indigenous bodies. Indeed, in our discussions of the incident, Deborah described the event as familiar and reminiscent of her own experiences. I wrote the following in my observational log a few days after the event:

> Yesterday, Crystal curled up against me when the vice-principal walked by us in the hall. She says she's fine but my overall impression is that she's somehow resigned to being treated this way? Deborah echoed this fear and wondered if <u>she</u> [Deborah] was behaving in this way as well.

Colonial order and control was and is maintained through a racial hierarchy. This reality, in turn, means that it is necessary that this book consider how such a racial hierarchy is created in a settler colony and what roles settler schools play in producing and reproducing such a hierarchy. This hierarchy:

> organized privileges, rights, and entitlements of juridical subjects through a race status actuated as essential and immutable. The native was defined not simply as ignorant of ethics, morals, and values (Christian or other), and native society as not only devoid of such values, but the native, and his /her society came to be constituted as the very 'negation' of these values, ethics, and morality. The colonial world emerged as a world divided: on the one hand, a world of law, privilege, access to wealth, status, and power for the settler; on the other, a world defined in *law* as being 'lawless,' a world of poverty, squalor, and death for the native. (Thobani, 2007: 37)

Defining Indigenous peoples in this way is what permitted settlers to become lawful and exalted members of settler nations. This system, in turn, gets reproduced because 'human beings internalize systems of repression and reproduce them by conforming to certain ideas of what is normal and what is deviant' (Loomba, 1998: 41). This societal mechanism, in part, is what allows colonialist thinking and systems to continue to operate and produce present-day societal inequities.

Nationalism, which we can think of as ideologies and discourses used as a way of mobilizing support for a nation, is one of the mechanisms that leads to the reproduction of the social structure. Stasiulis and Yuval-Davis (1995) argue that nationalist ideologies cannot be understood satisfactorily, especially those in settler societies, without also considering what Otto Bauer has called (the myth of) 'common destiny' (Stasiulis & Yuval-Davis, 1995: 19). In settler societies such as New Zealand, the present-day myth of common destiny is one of biculturalism. In Canada and Australia, the common destiny ideology is one of multiculturalism. The myth of common destiny implies an orientation to the future rather than the past which, in the case of heterogeneous settler societies, is very useful. Common destiny can account for:

> the subjective sense of commitment of people to ethnic collectivities and nations, in settler societies or in post-colonial states in which there is no one overriding shared myth of common origin. The myth of common destiny can also explain the dynamic nature of any national collectivity

and the perpetual reconstruction of boundaries which takes place within them via immigration, naturalization, conversion and other similar social and political processes. (Stasiulis & Yuval-Davis, 1995: 19)

Settler societies do not have racially or ethnically homogeneous populations; these are not elements that tie such societies together as nations. The myth of common destiny functions as a stabilizing factor for nation-building in diverse settler societies.

Settler societies also rely on 'foundational fictions' of expansion, conquest and settlement (Bhabha, 1990) to stabilize the national collective. This idea of 'foundation fictions' brings us back to the discussion of racial hierarchy. Settler societies such as Canada, Australia and Mexico consist of a range of racial and ethnic groups. Not surprisingly, the closer one is to the end of the spectrum that represents Western European settler, the closer one tends to be to 'a world of law, privilege, access to wealth, status, and power' (Thobani, 2007: 37). The story of how this hierarchy gets reproduced in each nation-state is complex and, again, differs from place to place. In Canada, Thobani argues that:

> The direct relation established between 'early explorers and settlers' and today's upstanding and responsible citizens becomes comprehensible only within the context of the continuity of their shared racial identity. Narrations of such mythological line of descent enable subsequent generations of Canadians to define themselves as repositories and preservers of the national inheritance, even as they make invisible the colonial violence which in actuality brought far more 'hardships' and 'dangers' to Native people than it did to 'early explorers and settlers'. The widespread race hatred expressed by the 'pioneers' who actively campaigned to prohibit the migration of Black and Asian immigrants, while they themselves were taking possession of the land, presented far more hardships and dangers to these migrants. (Thobani, 2007: 87)

Nation-building in Canada initially elevated British and French settlers over other Europeans, but the need for settling the country soon required (and requires) the immigration of other Europeans, as well as non-Europeans. The continuity of the 'shared racial identity' of European colonists and subsequent white settlers (Western and Eastern European) means that present-day white settlers remain elevated over non-European immigrants as well as Indigenous peoples and white settler ways of speaking English remained elevated over indigenized ways of performing English. In this way, our colonial past continues to produce the racial and linguistic hierarchy of the present.

Conclusion

The expansion of European nations to other spaces in this world was a project of the largest scale. European settlers built themselves new worlds and made themselves into new peoples. Colonialism originated in the encounters between Indigenous and European peoples; this contact created new categories of humans in colonial societies: the settler and the 'native'. Understanding the mechanisms of such a process as well as the impact of European imperialism on societies is no small feat. The goal of this chapter is to provide such an overview to foreground an understanding of linguistic bias as intimately entwined with colonial beliefs and practices made possible through European imperialism.

This chapter provides an overview of European imperialism and some of the mechanisms of settler nationalism, including colonial ideologies and discourses. Subsequent chapters continue this discussion by exploring the implications of these movements on the educational field as well as educational agents such as parents, teachers and students. Chapter 4 explores the historical constructions of race and nation in settler societies by focusing on the functions of these processes in the Canadian province where I live: Saskatchewan. The discussions in Chapter 4 extend the theoretical notions presented in this chapter's discussions of imperialism, colonialism and nationalism by using examples from the history of one particular settler society and the stories of one particular white settler girl – me – to demonstrate some of the ways in which colonial discourses and the resulting pedagogical activities of settler schools are involved in the reproduction of dominance.

4 Constructing Race in Settler Saskatchewan

Introduction

Chapter 3 discussed the processes of European expansion and settler colonialism and made connections between these movements and the types of beliefs about language that they engender. Chapter 6 focuses more closely on these connections through a discussion of data taken from my interviews with educators about their views on language. Before continuing with that more explicit discussion of language, I would like to discuss the discursive production of race and space in Chapters 4 and 5. Developing these types of understanding about the ways in which schools are involved in positioning people is a necessary precursor to understanding how the language varieties associated with settler and Indigenous groups of people are viewed in settler schools. As I explained in Chapter 3, the relationship between settler nationalism and language must be considered when examining educator linguistic bias. In spite of its relevance, the role that schools play in producing the nation, and the people who live within it, is something that we do not always think about in explicit ways.

Education is often seen as a source of upward movement or as simply a place where children receive knowledge and skills required for successful lives. Often ignored is the continuing role that schools play as a nationalizing force and all that this phrase implies in terms of the pedagogical practices necessary for producing homogeneity in a heterogeneous settler society. Because while schools may indeed be sites of knowledge-building, they are also places where students are socialized into views, behaviours and identities deemed as 'Canadian', 'grade-level', 'typical', 'standard', 'normal' and 'average' (to name a few of the terms we might use when describing what is viewed as appropriate ways of being in settler schools). In this chapter, I want to make explicit some of the ways that the movements of European imperialism and settler nationalism influence the field of education which, in turn, contributes to the production of the racial hierarchy of the nation.

Towards the goal of revealing the relationship between schools and discursive productions of race in settler societies, the ideas and events presented in this section draw on a review of relevant literature and personal narratives of my childhood memories of school. Using these sources of information, I discuss Saskatchewan's history of invasion and settlement as an example of a postcolonial rendering of colonial history, something sometimes referred to as a counter-history. By means of this counter-history, this chapter also examines the construction of race in this white settler society by examining how schools take up settler tales and the role that pedagogical practices play in reproducing racial hierarchies. Understanding the whiteness of schools allows us to better understand why Indigenized Englishes (and the speakers of these indigenized language varieties) are expelled (literally and figuratively) from these spaces.

In Canada, because of the strength and influence of multiculturalism as a common destiny myth, charges of racism and discrimination are controversial and often disputed. *Tolerance* as a form of multicultural discourse as well as the idea of a Canadian meritocracy means that many Canadians, white settlers in particular, are sometimes resistant to or deny issues of inequity along race lines (Thobani, 2007; Razack, 2002; Stasiulis & Yuval-Davis, 1995). In spite of (or perhaps because of) these skewed views of reality, Indigenous peoples experience institutional racism in educational systems, have higher levels of poverty within in their communities and are less likely to be employed and more likely to be incarcerated (Adams, 1999). In the Saskatchewan cities of Regina and Saskatoon and Winnipeg, a city in the neighbouring province, 60% of urban First Nations and Métis households live below the poverty line. In Regina, the city where I live at present, '81 per cent of Aboriginal households live in poverty and the high school drop out rate for Aboriginal children is 90 per cent – higher than in any other [Canadian] city' (Razack, 2002). Sherene Razack writes that:

> There are perhaps no better indicators of continuing colonization and its accompanying spatial strategies of containment than the policing and incarceration of urban Aboriginal peoples, a direct continuation of the policing relationship of the nineteenth century. Between the late 1960s and the early 1970s, the number of Aboriginal peoples in Regina's jails increased by 10 per cent. In 1971 the city stepped up downtown patrols, and in 1975 created a special task force for the purpose of policing Aboriginal peoples. (Razack, 2002: 133)

In 1991, Indigenous peoples comprised 12% of federal and 19% of provincial admissions, while only accounting for 2.5% of the Canadian population (Correctional Service of Canada, 2008). Corrections Canada also indicates that in 1995, while Indigenous peoples represented 10.8% of the population in Saskatchewan, they constituted 72.0% of Saskatchewan's provincial inmates; this was the highest level of incarceration of Indigenous peoples in Canada. The pervasive nature of institutional racism in Saskatchewan is further evidenced by a highly publicized incident that is likely illustrative of the relationship between Indigenous peoples and Saskatchewan police. A 2004 provincial inquiry into the 1990 death of Neil Stonechild, a 17-year-old First Nations man living in Saskatoon, confirmed that Stonechild had been apprehended by City of Saskatoon police and then abandoned outside the Saskatoon city limits. Stonechild froze to death in the −28 °C weather and investigations into this occurrence revealed that the Saskatoon Police's practice of leaving Indigenous peoples outside city limits, or giving someone 'the starlight tour', dates back to the 1970s (Commission of Inquiry into Matters Related to the Death of Neil Stonechild, 2004).

In contrast, the lived experiences of Saskatchewan's settler population are revealed in very different ways by statistics related to education and employment. In the Saskatchewan cities of Saskatoon and Regina, Indigenous peoples are three times as likely to be unemployed as settlers (Mendelson, 2004). If this ratio is compared to the federal capital region of Canada – Ottawa-Hull, where the indigenous unemployment rate is but 1.3 times that of the general population, the intensity of the racial imbalance in Saskatchewan becomes more apparent. Mendelson also makes reference to the high-school incompletion rate among Indigenous populations and explains that 'once again, we see a pattern of generally rising relative rates as we move from the east to the west, to reach their highest levels in Saskatchewan's cities and then diminish as we go further west' (Mendelson, 2004: 23). Politically, economically and socially, we see patterns of racial inequity for Indigenous peoples and racial bias towards white settlers in Saskatchewan society and societal institutions. This chapter examines some of the origins of this racial inequity; how it continues to be produced; and the role that settler schools play in exalting settler children like myself.

A Story of Conquest and Invasion

Saskatchewan's current social conditions and particular racial beliefs did not develop in some sort of vacuum only to be unleashed into Saskatchewan in 2011, the year in which I am writing this book. Taiaiake Alfred (1999), a Kanien'kehaka academic, argues that, 'without a good understanding of history, it is difficult to grasp how intense the European effort to destroy indigenous nations has been' (Alfred, 1999: 5). Similarly, Indigenous researchers Kathy Absolon and Cam Willet argue that 'any illumination of past, present, and future First Nations conditions demands a complete deconstruction of the history and application of ideology and, most importantly, of the impact (personal and political) of racism. That is, we need to know how we got into the mess we're in' (Absolon & Willet, 2004: 9). The Saskatchewan context that I describe in this book is framed in this destructive history and the statistics I provided in the introductory section to this chapter help to reveal the 'mess we're in.' Let me turn to a discussion of the past – distant and my own more recent – so we can better understand the effort that settlers have gone to in the subjugation of Indigenous peoples. Understanding these efforts will subsequently help us to understand similar levels of effort in the biased educational practices of settler schools.

I grew up in a small farming community of 900 people in the East-central area of my province. It has been my experience that many people often associate a small-town upbringing as a sheltered or innocent experience, one that might protect town inhabitants from having to consider the complicated societal processes that affect larger centres. Consider, however, the following statement:

> Small rural communities are hardly places of refuge from broader economic, cultural, and political forces. They never were. They exist on the Canadian prairies as a legacy of the National Policy, which made the territorial occupation of the region a primary purpose to be achieved through widespread agricultural settlement. (Epp, 2008: 49)

From this perspective, the story of my small-town childhood is actually one of colonial occupation. Not exactly an innocent start to life. Looking back, the adults of my childhood universe were, for the most part, themselves children of Eastern-European immigrants, socially conservative, Roman Catholic, farmers and labourers. Like most children, I did not spend a lot of time considering whether my circumstances were normal, I simply went about the life that was created for me by my parents and the adults of my community.

As the child of a teacher; as a student; as a teacher and as an educational researcher, I have literally been in school environments since birth. My life has always revolved around schools; my new 'year' begins in September (not January) and I often remember school experiences more clearly than other aspects of my life. I want to share a memory from my Grade 6 'year-end party' in 1985 that is linked to the stories of conquest and invasion that I tell in this chapter. Normally, a good year-end party meant a walk to the town sand pits or a swim and hotdogs with another class at our town pool. The year 1985 was also the centennial of the Métis resistance at Batoche or the *Riel Rebellion* as we were taught to call it. This uprising is a significant moment in Canadian history and because 1985 was the hundred-year anniversary of the 'Riel Rebellion', my class was able to travel by school bus to the site of the former Métis village of Batoche to see first-hand where the event occurred.

Before leaving on our trip, I remember our teacher explaining the significance of this Federal Heritage Site and why we were going to see it. As a child, I remember having a strong sensation that Canadian history was something that happened in Ontario and Quebec; these places were certainly the topic of most of my textbooks. On that day in Grade 6, I remember being excited to finally see an important Canadian place in my own province. Similarly, I can still remember our collective disappointment when we arrived at Batoche to find a camper-trailer being used as a temporary information centre and one guide who offered to take us on a walking tour of a prairie field and a graveyard. Today, Batoche is home to a wonderful interpretive centre complete with multimedia centre, museum, guided tours and bilingual staff. At the time, I simply remember thinking that a party at the sandpits was not such a bad idea after all.

The beginning of Saskatchewan's shared history between Indigenous peoples and white settlers finds its roots in what is today the Canadian province of Manitoba at an important trading centre which was then known as Red River. Until the 1860s, the Hudson's Bay Company held constitutional authority over the Northwest Territories, today's Canadian prairie provinces. Canadian industrialists and British financiers had comfortably secured their place in Eastern Canada and were looking west to the land and resources of the Northwest Territories. Their desires were in opposition to Hudson Bay's economic system and conflict was inevitable. This collision of interests would fuel the 1869–1870 clash that is today commonly referred to as the *Red River Rebellion* or, as Howard Adams calls it, the *Red River Resistance*. Adams also indicates that while this resistance is commonly billed as a conflict between the Métis and Ottawa, at the heart of the matter actually lay the conflict between the two economic systems. To summarize, this important event is complicated. Essentially, the Métis and First Nations of the Red River, led by Louis Riel, decided to protect their interests and way of life and resist the colonial powers of Ottawa. As Adams maintains, the Hudson's Bay Company found it easiest to hide behind the Métis movement and simply allow the Métis to engage in the conflict rather than representing themselves and their economic interests in battle.

In 1868, the British government ceded the Northwest Territories to Ottawa and a group of several hundred soldiers was sent west to enforce this exchange. When the forces arrived, it was clear to Riel that it was futile to resist. Adams (1989) explains that Ottawa's some 400 troops arrived and violently seized the land and goods of the Red River Métis. In 1870, left with nothing, many of the Red River Métis moved west and joined a small settlement on the South Saskatchewan River called Batoche, the site I visited for my Grade 6 trip. Here, they built a life very similar to the one in the Red River settlement.

After the events of Red River, the ensuing development of the Canadian prairies reads like a how-to manual for the colonization and subjugation of a people. Stasiulis and Jhappan (1995) explain the need for coercive measures 'in the effort to obliterate Aboriginal and mixed-race communities in order to open the prairies to white settlement' (Stasiulis & Jhappan, 1995: 114). The Canadian government wanted control of what would become Saskatchewan's land and, therefore, needed to avoid a repeat of the troublesome Métis uprisings of 1870. The British North America Act of 1867 gave jurisdiction over Indigenous peoples and land reserved for them to the federal government. The introduction of the Indian Act in 1876 consolidated all pre-existing legislation and created a 'totalitarian "cradle-to-grave" set of rules, regulations and directives to manage Native lives' (Stasiulis & Jhappan, 1995: 114).

The urgency of preventing further uprisings similar to the 1870 resistance event at Red River led to the creation of the Royal Northwest Mounted Police in 1873 and to the establishment of a training centre in Regina, Saskatchewan, a facility which remains to this day (Adams, 1999). Next in Ottawa's plans to push west was the building of the Canadian Pacific Railroad. In order to accomplish this goal, it was necessary first to seize the land of the plains First Nations and confine them to reserves of land. Adams (1989) posits that, like the government of the United States, it is possible that the Canadian government played a role in depleting the buffalo herds. This is significant as the loss of the buffalo, in turn, led to drastic changes in the Indigenous peoples' ways of life. Starving, linguistically disadvantaged and unable to resist Ottawa's forces, First Nations were left with little other choice than to sign unfair treaties that endowed with them with few rights and goods, little power, money or land, which would strip them of their way of life. Today, there are 72 reserves, or First Nations as they are now known, in Saskatchewan. First Nations comprise only about 1% of the provincial land base (Government of Saskatchewan, 2009).

At roughly the same time as First Nations were being stripped of their ways of life, conflict developed again between Ottawa and the Métis (and their First Nations allies), now living at Batoche. In 1885, they clashed a second time over land-parcelling, language and customs in a series of battles and strategic manoeuvres that finally ended with casualties of hundreds for the First Nations and Métis (Adams, 1989). After this second resistance, Ottawa chose to send a strong message to all people in Saskatchewan by publicly hanging nine Indigenous peoples and imprisoning 44. Bumsted explains the importance of those events and of the year of 1885 to the expansion of the Canadian West in the following citation:

> The military defeat of the Métis, the public execution of Louis Riel in November 1885 for treason, and the campaign of repression against the First Nations supplied only half the reason why that year (and even that month) was so significant, not only in the history of the West but in the history of Canada. For in November of 1885, the last spike was driven at Craigellachie in eastern British Columbia to mark the completion of the Canadian Pacific Railway. (Bumsted, 2001: 316)

Ottawa's triumph at Batoche dehumanized the Métis sufficiently so as to effectively limit them, financially and emotionally, to living in poverty-stricken ghettos. Similarly, First Nations were confined to reserves where they required the permission of an Indian agent to leave their community. Stasiulis and Jhappan explain how this was achieved and maintained:

> Key to the federal policies of Indian protection and assimilation was a pass law which forbade departure from official reserve lands without the permission of government-appointed Indian agents. In effect from 1885 to 1930, this system became the model for the infamous pass and homelands system, central element in racial apartheid in South Africa. (Stasiulis & Jhappan, 1995: 115)

With a coast-to-coast railroad in place, the prairies were available for development and, thus, to complete its expansion westward, the Canadian Confederation worked very hard to establish European settlements throughout the province. Many white settlers, including my grandparents, came to Saskatchewan because of the Canadian Government's promise of free land, and because of conflict and poverty in their home countries, countries the Canadian Government targeted with promises of prosperity and freedom in Canada. Like many settler children, I grew up with stories of how my grandparents 'came over' and 'homesteaded the land'. It is striking to me now that these pioneer tales I so enjoyed as a child are actually stories of invasion, settlement and displacement.

From 1879 to 1986, while white settlers were 'developing' the west, thousands of Indigenous children were moving through the residential school system; many of whom were forcibly removed from their homes. Milloy (1999) tells us that the government's goal for these schools was to bring Indigenous children into the 'circle of civilization'. It is now common knowledge that what these schools produced was a dismal education in an abusive and neglectful environment. Children were underfed, beaten for speaking their Indigenous languages and were physically and sexually abused. Milloy argues that residential schools 'have been, arguably, the most damaging of the many elements of Canada's colonization of this land's original peoples and, as their consequences still affect the lives of Aboriginal people today, they remain so' (Milloy, 1999: xiv).

Looking back over the past 150 years through a postcolonial lens, the building blocks of Saskatchewan's current racial inequity are obvious. Initially, Indigenous peoples were stripped of land as imperial institutions of domination such as the Royal Northwest Mounted Police were put in place. Next, First Nations were confined to reserves and white settlers acquired their seized land. Subsequently, First Nations children were processed through the brutal machine of assimilation, the residential school system. All of these components of Saskatchewan's history share the common goal of maintaining control and power over land and resources. How does this history continue to shape the identities of those of us who live here?

Becoming White by Learning about Others

Let me take you back again to my Grade 6 year, in my town roughly two hours away (in rural Saskatchewan, we measure distance in driving time) from the site of the Riel Resistance. In school that year, my classmates and I also learned about 'The Plains Indians' in Social Studies. Our teacher placed us in groups to work on presentations of the different First Nations groups that we had been assigned. I do not remember which First Nations my group was given, but I do remember giggling and stumbling over their seemingly 'foreign' names. I have a happy memory of creating a giant map of Saskatchewan on a piece of paper on the classroom wall. This map was easily produced by an overhead projector as we only had to remember that our province was 'in the shape of a skirt.' I can recall how strangely pleased and proud we all were that our province had none of the complicated natural borders of Alberta or Manitoba. At that time, I was unaware of the complicated national history that had created those artificial borders that were so easy for us to draw with the aid of a ruler.

I am not sure that I made the connection between the people about whom we were learning and the Indigenous peoples who lived in my community when I was in Grade 6. Adams (1989) explains that, after 1885, white settler colonialists forcibly ossified Indigenous peoples' culture and society. Looking back, this ossification is visible in my Social Studies curriculum. The First Nations' customs, cultures and languages that we learned and presented about were those of the late 19th century, a way of life that had been stolen because of the economic desires of the newly confederated Canada (Adams, 1989). It was as if time had stopped in 1885, Indigenous peoples had ceased to exist, or more specifically, that they had ceased to matter. There was no discussion of racial inequity, issues of poverty or discrimination that were, quite literally, in front of our eyes. Instead, 'the Plains Indian' was presented as a lesson about the past. This relegating of First Nations to the past through school curriculum is not limited to my classroom experiences. Consider, for example, the following statement by Roger Epp about his daughter's reaction after attending a pow-wow in the Canadian prairies:

> I have brought my children to a pow-wow in the community, after which my daughter confessed surprise that 'there were so many of them,' having received an impression in her elementary school curriculum of the demise of a people. (Epp, 2008: 136)

In my province, Indigenous peoples tend to be represented, essentialized and othered in two ways: (a) through archaic cultural and exotic representations that my class learned about which included, but were certainly not limited to, teepees, buffalo hunts and peace pipes and (b) as a morally bankrupt and socially inferior race of people. Adams' (1989) description of the nature of a town where Saskatchewan's two solitudes live side-by-side highlights this second racial stereotype painfully well:

> There are always two distinct communities. The native section has no gas or running water, no paved streets or sidewalks, only trails and dirt roads. Many of the houses are one- or two-room shacks. The differences are more than economic and cultural, they are vividly racial. According to the whites, the native section is a place of lazy, diseased, and evil people incapable of doing anything for themselves, a breeding ground for violence. The whites claim that natives have no culture, no ethics, no sensibility to morality, and no appreciation of law and order. To these colonizers, Indians and Métis destroy and disfigure beauty. The whites speak of their neighbours in bestial terms, complaining that 'they breed like rabbits.' They speak of the sinful and depraved behavior of natives, of shacking-up, of common-law marriages, of sleeping around. (Adams, 1989: 41)

While these words may seem harsh, the types of discourses about Indigenous peoples described by Adams were openly expressed by white settlers in Saskatchewan when I was in Grade 6 and continue to circulate today. While many of the adults in my childhood community might have believed this stereotype to be true, it would have been difficult to find one who would openly admit to it. Masking or hiding such views persists today. Indeed, a 2004 survey conducted by the *Regina Leader Post*, a provincial newspaper, indicates that 67% of Saskatchewanians agree or strongly agree that it is difficult to openly discuss Indigenous issues. In that newspaper article, Brock Pitawanakwat, an Indigenous Studies professor at First Nations University in Regina interprets this statistic in two ways: (a) it is possible that people do not feel they know enough to speak openly about their opinions or (b) people keep their socially unaccepted opinions to themselves (Rhodes, 2004). I would be willing to place my bets on the latter.

Saskatchewanians do not feel comfortable discussing contemporary issues related to Indigenous peoples (Rhodes, 2004). In my classroom in 1985, we did not talk about the First Nations and Métis children in our elementary school. Nobody asked why our schoolmates did not dress or behave like the Indigenous peoples presented in our textbooks. We did not travel to a First Nation, an unthinkable excursion even though the closest was just over an hour away. Our teacher did not invite First Nations elders to come visit us nor, more importantly, did he lead us in any critical discussion of colonialism or its enduring effects on Indigenous peoples and white settlers. These activities would have been inconceivable mainly because the view of Indigenous peoples as socially inferior to white settlers, is the perception that many people in my town held.

Adams argues that the image of the 'Noble Savage' is more comfortable for white settlers because it corresponds to the stereotype of the authentic Indigenous peoples (Adams, 1989: 36). This image also allows us to distance ourselves from our complicity in creating the social ills and subjugation experienced by Indigenous peoples. In my sixth-grade class, to learn about the Indigenous peoples who live in Saskatchewan, my classmates and I lay on our cool, tiled classroom floor, coloured our maps, carefully added the North and South Saskatchewan rivers, and copied outdated information about the Cree, Saulteaux or another nation from the Encyclopedia Britannica. As an educator, I can guess that the pedagogical goals of this particular activity might have been to provide us with knowledge about the original inhabitants of Saskatchewan; what educators sometimes call 'including Aboriginal content' to the curriculum. As a critical researcher, I would argue that there was a more important, but hidden, objective to our unit on 'The Plains

Indian,' one that as 11-year-olds, my classmates and I could not have understood but that we nonetheless internalized.

The old ways of 'The Plains Indian' became obsolete, something only to be studied, when Europeans arrived in Canada. The underlying message of the unit was that Europeans introduced and continue to maintain civility in Canada. Cree educator Angelina Weenie explains that 'European supremacy is based on the civilized/uncivilized dichotomy, and it effectively justifies colonization. The colonizers are depicted as the advanced civilization, while the colonized are depicted as backward nations' (Weenie, 2000: 66). The creation of such a dichotomy between the colonizer and the colonized allows settlers to feel justified in the dominance and control of the colonized people. Introducing settler children to this dichotomy through pedagogical activities that teach them to see themselves as civilized and Indigenous peoples as a savage blip on a development timeline is part of how settler children take up whiteness, including myself.

While Gramsci's concept of *hegemony* was not accessible to me at the age of 11, it is this notion that probably best describes the lessons that we learned in our Grade 6 classroom. We were taught that the cultural forms and ideas of the Europeans who came to Canada are preferable and, therefore, as white settler descendants of Europeans, our domination over Indigenous peoples is justified. I learned that the Canadian prairies were devoid of any meaningful human civilization prior to contact; received little information about treaties; understood the Métis resistance at Batoche to be a rebellion, and received no information regarding residential schools or the slavery of Indigenous peoples in Canada. I have come to understand the pedagogical experiences I describe here as decidedly Eurocentric. While messages of racial superiority were not spoken aloud, through our lessons on 'The Plains Indian' and our rural Saskatchewan childhoods, we were socialized into our positions of privilege and the comfortable knowledge that we were part of the superior and civilized race of Saskatchewan. Alarmingly, these types of lessons and the racialized bodies they produce are ongoing in Saskatchewan classrooms (Sterzuk & Mulholland, 2011).

Why White Settlers Need to Dominate Others

The previous sections explored Saskatchewan's colonial history as well as some of the pedagogical activities of my childhood that demonstrate ways in which schools potentially contribute to the construction of racial identities. The historical context in which schools are grounded helps to produce the present-day context in which white settlers enjoy economic, political and social privilege, and Indigenous peoples continue to resist and struggle against colonialist ideologies and structures. This section explores the ways in which racial domination continues to be necessary for white settlers to continue to benefit economically and socially. Schick and St Denis (2003: 62) explain that the white identity requires a subjugated partner against which their 'own whiteness and goodness' is understood. In Saskatchewan, racial inequity between white settlers and Indigenous peoples is the result of a carefully choreographed dance, constructed by over a century and a half of colonial activity.

In my province, there exists a strong myth of meritocracy – the idea that equal access to success is achievable for all. In effect, many white settlers in Saskatchewan believe that one can achieve success through hard work and perseverance. These ideologies manifest themselves in discourses about pioneer grit; the prairie work ethic; and our 'barn-raising mentality'. These beliefs are intrinsically linked to how whiteness came to be constructed in Saskatchewan. Schick and St Denis (2003) explain that 'whiteness refers to a set of locations that are historically, socially, politically, and culturally produced and moreover are intrinsically linked to unfolding relations of domination' (Schick & St Denis, 2003: 6). Schick describes whiteness in Saskatchewan as a 'particular shade of white' and I think this imagery is useful in exploring how white settlers came to have their unearned privilege and why the subjugation of Indigenous peoples is necessary for white settlers to maintain their exalted positions (Thobani, 2007).

As I mentioned earlier, many settlers who initially came to Saskatchewan were not from England or France but came from Eastern European places known today as Germany, Hungary and Ukraine (to name a few). The ways of life that these settlers brought with them were seen by British-Canadians to be 'rife with violence, pagan excess and idleness' (Stasiulis & Jhappan, 1995: 111). As they were for First Nations and Métis students, Saskatchewan schools were used as a tool of assimilation for these off-white settlers. In the early 1900s, the Saskatchewan Department of Education made a propaganda film called *The Education of New Canadians* about 'what Saskatchewan is doing for Canadianization in the West.' I was fortunate enough to be introduced to this film by my colleague Dr Carol Schick. The film, a presentation of the nation to itself, shows clips of young 'Ruthenian, German, Polish and Bohemian' children and explains that 'if we are to build up a strong and unified Canadian people in the great Dominion, we must solve the problem of racial assimilation' (Saskatchewan Department of Education, 1917). 'Canadianization' programmes such as the ones presented in this video were necessary to assimilate these off-white races. In response, non-Anglo-Saxon immigrants to Saskatchewan anglicized last names (My grandfather clearly could have done a better job of this. The 'zuk' in my last name is a dead giveaway); eschewed the ways and languages of their old countries; and acculturated to the newly shared culture of Saskatchewan. The pay-off was that these ethnic minority white settlers, like my father's family, got to become a paler shade of white in the process.

Saskatchewan white settlers' 'toehold on respectability' is 'dependant upon their construction of themselves as not-Other' (Schick, 2002: 103). A constructed (and carefully maintained) dichotomy of white respectability and indigenous criminality is necessary for us to be certain of our whiteness. As members of a white ethnic minority that is a slightly different shade of white than a British white settler, white ethnic minority settlers in Saskatchewan 'claim their entitlement by moving closer to the centre of white norms and values by means of "dominance through difference"' (Schick, 2002: 104).

In an earlier chapter, I introduced Schick and St Denis' discussion paper regarding pre-service teachers in Saskatchewan universities which outlines and examines three commonly held ideological assumptions regarding racial inequality: '(1) race does not matter; (2) everyone has equal opportunity; and (3) through individual acts and good intentions one can secure innocence as well as superiority' (Schick & St Denis, 2003: 1). In the authors' anti-racism classes, they describe resistance of their white settler undergraduate students in discussions of racial inequality. Denying racial inequality is a characteristic of white settler societies (Razack, 2002). By denying that race matters and that racial inequality exists, the privilege of white settlers disappears; it becomes invisible.

Riley and Ungerleider explored the judgements of students in a Canadian teacher education programme. This study examined whether pre-service teachers make discriminatory judgements about the potential of settler and Indigenous students. In this study, participants were asked to make decisions about 24 students based on records of past performance in a number of school subjects. These records also 'provided a subtle clue about the student's background as either a student of Aboriginal ancestry (Aboriginal), a student for whom English was a second language (ESL), or a student who was neither of Aboriginal ancestry nor one for whom English was a second language (non-Aboriginal)' (Riley & Ungerleider, 2008: 381). Using a scale of 1–10, study participants were asked to determine the appropriate programme (remedial, standard or advanced) for each of the 24 students. In their analysis of the data, Riley and Ungerleider compared recommendations of 'Aboriginal students and non-Aboriginal students at each achievement (GPA) level' (Riley & Ungerleider, 2008: 383). Despite identical student records of prior achievement, 'Aboriginal students consistently earned lower recommendations than their non-Aboriginal counterparts' (Riley & Ungerleider, 2008: 383). What the results of this study reveal are the potential role of schools and educators in perpetuating racial inequity and the power of colonialist discourses which circulate throughout societies.

Cummins (2000) defines institutional racism as 'ideologies and structures which are systematically used to legitimize unequal division of power and resources between groups which are defined on the basis of race' (Cummins, 2000: 131). Practices employed by Saskatchewan schools, employers, police forces and the judiciary system – often seen as common sense – are used to legitimize inequity and reinforce the racial binary construct between Indigenous peoples and white settlers. By denying that racial inequality exists and by perpetuating the belief that success (educational, economic and social) is merit based, white settlers are able to legitimize their power, privilege and whiteness.

Conclusion

The arguments presented in this chapter draw on a review of relevant literature and my personal experiences growing up in Saskatchewan. With one of the main arguments from CRT in mind, the goal of this chapter was to examine just how 'race matters' in this province. The chapter began with a postcolonial rending of the past 150 years of Saskatchewan's history, with a focus on events, issues and motives related to land seizure, the creation of the Royal Canadian Mounted Police (RCMP), First Nations' confinement to reserves, and white settlements of seized land and residential schools. With the goal of understanding the role of school and curriculum in the construction of race in Saskatchewan, this chapter included some of my childhood memories of school, used as a way of demonstrating the implications of pedagogy beyond the transmission of knowledge.

As I explained in Chapter 1, one of the reasons for including my childhood memories in this chapter was to allow space for the discussion of some of the colonial discourses that circulate in settler schools to consider the impact of these discourses on the product of racial domination. Colonial discourses such as terra nullius and myths of common destiny continue to reproduce the racial hierarchy I described in Chapter 3. Developing an understanding of how white settlers can be discursively constructed through contact with 'coming over' tales of 'pioneer grit' and pedagogical activities that convey a view of pre-contact North America as being as the absence of civilization is important in terms of understanding educator views of indigenized Englishes in settler spaces like schools. Chapter 5 continues this chapter's consideration of race through its discussion of the racialization of school and urban spaces.

5 The Racialization of Space and School in Settler Saskatchewan

Introduction

Sherene Razack argues that 'mythologies of white settler societies are deeply spatialized stories' (Razack, 2002: 3). This idea was not necessarily obvious to me when I began my research. Throughout my research project, however, spatial configurations became more significant for me as I observed school activities, interviewed students and educators, and participated in school field trips outside the classroom. I began to understand that the boundaries of racialized spaces affect the lived school experiences and identities of educators, children and parents in a number of significant ways. This relationship between space and racial identity became an important aspect of my study both in terms of understanding how schools become white spaces and in terms of analysing which English language varieties are viewed as legitimate (and who has authority over them) in the white spaces of schools. Because of the impact of racialized spaces on my research and on the lived experiences of my research participants, it is necessary to examine how the colonial project discussed in the previous chapter manifests itself in the racialization of space. That is, it is important to better understand just how 'place becomes race' (Razack, 2002: 1).

Using the work of authors such as Henri Lefebvre, Razack argues convincingly that colonized societies are spatially configured. Her position is worth summarizing and sharing in terms of the discussion presented in this chapter. Razack describes the spatial story of colonialism in three phases. First, as discussed in Chapter 3, the relationship between law, race and land is revealed in the legal doctrine of terra nullius or the idea that land was empty or uninhabited if the people were not Christian or agricultural. A second phase of Canada's spatialized story is the mythology that exists around the empty land being developed by hardworking European settlers, a story implicit in the pedagogical activities of my childhood discussed in the previous chapter. Images of rugged landscapes and Canadian anthems that sing of the 'True North Strong and Free' are symbolic elements of the relationship between colonialism and space. Finally, space continues to be racially spatialized through stories of borders 'now besieged and crowded by Third World refugees and migrants who are drawn to Canada by the legendary niceness of European Canadians, their well-known commitment to democracy, and the bounty of their land. The "crowds" at the border threaten the calm, ordered spaces of the original inhabitants' (Razack, 2002: 4).

Razack's arguments around Canada and its history of racial spatialization allow her to 'denaturalize geography by asking how spaces come to be' (Razack, 2002: 5). This unmapping of colonized lands, Razack argues, is 'intended to undermine the idea of white settler innocence (the notion that European settlers merely settled and developed the land) and to uncover the ideologies and practices of conquest and domination' (Razack, 2002: 5). Like Razack's work, this chapter seeks to unmap some of the ways that schools contribute to the creation of racialized spaces in urban Saskatchewan as a continuation of the colonial project described in the previous chapter. Razack explains this process in this way:

> In unmapping, there is an important relationship between identity and space. What is being imagined or projected on to specific spaces and bodies, and what is being enacted there? Who do white citizens know themselves to be and how much does an identity of dominance rely upon keeping racial Others firmly *in place*? How are people kept in their place? And, finally how does place become race? We ask these questions here in the fervent belief that white settler societies can transcend their bloody beginnings and contemporary inequalities by remembering and confronting the racial hierarchies that structure our lives. (Razack, 2002: 5)

This section draws heavily on Razack's work by asking these same questions in regards to the settler school and community in which I conducted my research. How did this school's neighbourhood become the 'inner city?' Why do the white settlers who teach at that school not actually live in the school neighbourhood? How do schools come to be white spaces? Why does this all seem so 'natural?' By drawing on observations noted in my logbooks, interviews and conversations with educators and children and some of my personal experiences in the school and community, this chapter explores: (a) the geographical boundaries in the community; (b) white settler strategies for maintaining racialized spaces; and (c) some of the ways in which children are socialized into perpetuating the spatialization.

East Side Meets West Side

The community where I conducted my research is divided into the 'West Side' and the 'East Side' by a river that splits the city into two. In general, the East Side of the city is considered to be affluent, safe and the area of the city where middle and upper class white settlers live. In contrast, the West Side is where we find the small downtown core, the inner city neighbourhoods and residential areas populated mainly by First Nations, Métis and working class white settlers. Curiously, the more affluent residential and commercial developments in the Northwest area of the city are not considered to be part of the West Side even though this area is, indeed, located west of the river. The terms 'West Side' and 'East Side' are not simply geographical markers; they convey messages about the class, race and culture of the people who live in those areas. Razack speaks about the relationship between identity and space. Messages about the 'West Side' and the 'East Side' are 'imagined or projected on to' the bodies of those who work and live in these spaces (Razack, 2002: 5). Here, I begin the work of unmapping the racialization of the school neighbourhood in which I conducted my research.

In Chapter 4, I discussed the confinement of First Nations to reserves of land. Before continuing with this discussion about the effects of spatial configuration, let me provide some more information about First Nations in-migration from reserves to cities. Razack explains that the 'nineteenth-century spatial containment of Aboriginal peoples [through the pass system] to reserves remained in place until the 1950s' (Razack, 2002: 131). By the 1960s, though, the spatialization of urban settler Canada changed because of a steady migration of Aboriginal peoples from reserves. Razack explains that a number of factors contributed to this stream of in-migration but highlights the role of federal cutbacks to housing budgets for reserves. Between the period of 1986 and 1991, 'the urban Aboriginal population in Canada increased by 55 per cent in contrast to the non-Aboriginal urban population increase of 11 per cent' (Razack, 2002: 132). The Canadian cities of Winnipeg, Manitoba and Regina and Saskatoon, Saskatchewan experienced higher rates of in-migration than other cities in Canada.

And yet, regardless of this in-migration and the increased presence of Aboriginal peoples in these Canadian prairie cities, 'Aboriginal people also remain outside the city's economy' (Razack, 2002: 133). In Winnipeg, Regina and Saskatoon, 'according to the 1991 census, 60 per cent of urban Aboriginal households live below the poverty line and, for single-parent households headed by women, the figure is 80 to 90 per cent' (Razack, 2002: 133). Unfortunately, this reality of 'remaining outside the city's economy' continues to the present day. Results from the 2006 census indicate that, in

Saskatchewan, the First Nations and Métis provincial unemployment rate was 18.2% compared to the settler unemployment rate of 4.2%. And a 2007 report issued by Statistics Canada indicates the following: 'in Saskatchewan, even though that province had the highest overall employment rate for persons aged 25 to 54, Aboriginal people do not appear to have benefited as much from the strong labour market in 2007. Saskatchewan was the province with the largest gap in employment rates between the Aboriginal and non-Aboriginal people' (Statistics Canada, 2007).

Razack explains that 'the spatial configuration of the nineteenth century and the social hierarchies it both engenders and sustains remain firmly embedded in the white Canadian psyche and in social and economic institutions' (Razack, 2002: 133). When I confirmed my research site and explained to my friends and family where I would be for three months of my study, I was teased about my safety in the school neighbourhood. Prior to beginning my study, jokes about gangs, drugs and bar shootings pervaded these conversations. Having grown up in this province, I knew, as they did, that this racialized space did not project itself onto my body or identity in the same way it would a First Nations or Métis person. My identity was tied to the white spaces of the East-Side community where I lived during my research; my settler hometown and the schools and universities where I studied. It was during an interview that I conducted with Larissa, a First Nations educational assistant-in-training, that I first began to think more about Saskatchewan's racialized spaces and what the teasing (and more serious queries about my safety) implied about the racialization of inner-city spaces and the bodies that did and did not belong there.

Andrea: The reason I ask is part of the stuff I write about is um the culture conflict or divide between First Nations and whites in Saskatchewan, how the two groups don't really mix, even to the point of in this city like you know what areas like where white people live and where First Nations people live, like it's not as clear as that, like there's people who live wherever, but in general there's this huge divide between the two groups
Larissa: The river
Andrea: Yeah
Larissa: [laughter]
Andrea: Pretty much, yeah eh?
Larissa: Yeah, cause when I started school, they [her college classmates] said 'So where do you live' they thought I lived around the West Side, 'The East Side' 'Why do you live on the East Side? You're supposed to live on the West Side', I was like 'Okay then'

When I began speaking to this participant about the divide between Indigenous peoples and white settlers, I had something more philosophical in mind. I was surprised when Larissa so clearly verbalized the real and important role the river plays in geographically dividing the two communities. This participant was originally from a northern area of Saskatchewan and had moved to the city to attend college. Like any newcomer to any community, she was unaware of the community norms surrounding where white settlers and Indigenous peoples typically live. As she explained in our interview, it was assumed by her classmates that she would have chosen to rent her apartment on the West Side because she is First Nations. The statement made by one of her classmates 'you're supposed to live on the West Side' expresses this community norm and expectation and alludes to her out-of-place-ness in terms of living in a white space.

After this interview, I began to pay more attention to how this neighbourhood is perceived by the community. In my interview with Corrine, a white settler educator, she describes some of the ways that the school and surrounding community are perceived by the larger city community:

Andrea: Community members in the city, how would they describe this school?

Corrine: Oh, oh my God, you work there? [Laughter] It's like 'whoa'

Andrea: Yeah? Is it considered among the worst?

Corrine: It's considered an inner city school and that's it, I don't think it's that bad but lots of people, there'd be no way they would work here, you know, there'd be no way they'd work here

Andrea: Is that because of the student population or because of the area?

Corrine: I'm not sure, I think it's both, the area and the student population, yeah, and the perceptions out there of this area and there's a lot of really negative perceptions of this area

Andrea: So would you think that that kind of city perception of this school would affect how teachers feel about working here?

Corrine: Oh probably after a while yeah and I think it affects the way the community, the parents see the school, the kids see the school

As I explained in the introductory chapter to this book, the school of this study is located in a poor neighbourhood and life is undeniably difficult for residents in many ways related to socioeconomic factors. This does not necessarily mean that teaching or working in a school in this neighbourhood is an unpleasant experience. In my time spent in the school, I witnessed many wonderful exchanges between students and teachers and heard many educators describe their work in favourable tones. Yet, Corrine's statement indicates that the school's reputation in the city is that it is dangerous or unpleasant to work at this school because of its neighbourhood or its students. The neighbourhood and school are constructed as a site of criminality, a place where the majority feel like 'there'd be no way they'd work there.'

A statement made by Elaine, the school principal, echoes Corrine's description of how city community members view this school and its students and families. The principal of this school is a white settler and lives in the East Side of the city. What follows is a statement taken from an interview with her:

> I thought I had a bit of a sense, you know, until you get over into this community, and these community, into community schools, I don't think you have any idea sense of what's going on and now when I listen to [my] friends and neighbours talking, you really, now it really hits me just how much they don't get it and there's so much good here and they don't get that, they don't get the poverty issues, there's a real sense, well people control their own destiny.

The closing line of the above excerpt is especially telling. Those who live in the more affluent areas of the city choose to believe that 'people control their own destiny.' The reality is more complex than a matter of choice or free will. Through reference to the work of David Goldberg, Razack explains that:

> At the end of the colonial era, and particularly with urbanization in the 1950s and 1960s, the segregation of urban spaces replaces these earlier [colonial] spatial practices: slum administration replaces colonial administration. The city belongs to the settlers and the sullying of civilized society through the presence of the racial Other in white space gives rise to a careful management of boundaries within urban space. Planning authorities require large plots in the suburbs, thereby ensuring that larger homes and wealthier families live there. Projects and Chinatowns are created, cordoning off the racial poor. Such spatial practices, often achieved through law (nuisance laws, zoning laws and so on), mark off the spaces of the settler and the native both conceptually and materially. The inner city is a racialized space, the zone in which all that is not respectable is contained. Canada's colonial geographies exhibit this same pattern of violent expulsions and the spatial containment of Aboriginal peoples to marginalized areas of the city, processes consolidated over three hundred years of colonization. (Razack, 2002: 129)

Settlers, like the friends Elaine describes in her excerpt, maintain that the racial poor *choose* to live in the economically depressed areas of the West Side. Living in the inner city in urban Canada is not, however, a matter of choice or free will but, rather, a racialized story that has evolved over centuries of colonization.

The children who attend the school where I conducted my research live just west of the river that divides this city in half. Some of them rarely, if ever, travel to the East Side but they are able to see it from across the river. Naively, I did not, at first, realize that they were aware of the divisive nature of the river or that the East Side is considered superior to the West Side. In a conversation with Starr, a First Nations child, I began to understand that the children of this neighbourhood, even at a young age, understand how their area of the city compares to the East Side.

Starr: Can't go in back alleys at night-time, can't go far away from home but me and my friend do, all the time, we went across the river once

Andrea: Across the river?

Starr: Yeah

Andrea: On what bridge?

Starr: Hamilton Bridge

Andrea: On that scary bridge? You went across?

Starr: I said to her and she was like 'I'm not going on Hamilton Bridge.' I said 'We're going on Hamilton Bridge or traintrack bridge' and then she said, 'Let's go across'

Andrea: You made her go?

Starr: She went after me and she says 'Is that where we're going cause it looks scary to me' and then I'm like 'Hurry up'

We continued to discuss her trip across the bridge to the East Side and I asked Starr what made her want to bike across to the other side. She explained to me that she had heard about the good parks on the other side of the river and wanted to see what they were like. By age nine, Starr seems fully aware of her inner-city space and of the affluency attached to the white spaces across the river.

The previous interview excerpts highlight the geographic divide between the West and East Sides of the city. Additionally, the interviewees' comments indicate that the members of the city community generally perceive the school and surrounding neighbourhood to be an undesirable and dangerous place to live and work. This segregation is geographically created by the river that separates the West Side from the affluent East Side of the city populated.

In addition to the role the river plays, white settler parents and, eventually, their children are invested in policing and maintaining the racial specialization of community and school. The next section explores some of the ways and why that white settlers work to maintain the whiteness of 'official' spaces like schools.

Keeping Things White: Settler Resistance to Violations of Racialized Boundaries

The city's urban planning website indicates that homes in the school neighbourhood have an average selling price in the range of $53,170–59,542. These numbers contrast drastically with the city's average home selling price of $124,514 in 2006. The lower cost of real estate in the school neighbourhood has led to some gentrification of the neighbourhood, specifically in areas closer to the river and further south of the school. This change means that there are some lower-middle-class white settler families living in the area that surrounds the school. Yet, while there are white settlers and Indigenous peoples living in the neighbourhood, white settlers have developed strategies to resist inter-group interaction and to keep legitimate spaces, like their children's schools, white.

In the neighbourhood where I conducted my research, there are two elementary schools to choose from: the school where I conducted my research and another school within a short distance. Additionally, there is a Catholic school further south of the neighbourhood. In the school which is the focus of my study, roughly 67% of students self-identify as First Nations or Métis. In the other neighbourhood school, Vincent Brown (a pseudonym), nearly 90% of students self-identify as First Nations or Métis. During my three months in the school where I conducted my research, I observed and discussed with interviewees some of the ways in which white settler parents in the neighbourhood resist the presence of Indigenous educators in schools as well as how they avoid sending their children to schools with a high number of First Nation and Métis students. These discussions inform this section of the chapter. Some of the ways in which white settler parents' and community members' strategies and behaviour affect Indigenous educators in the school where I conducted my research are also discussed. Finally, this section explores how these strategies of resistance as used by white settlers contribute to the maintenance of racialized spaces in this settler city.

The easiest way for white settler parents to circumvent having their children come into contact with Indigenous students or educators is simply to avoid sending them to one of the two neighbourhood schools. This can be accomplished by simply choosing to enrol one's child in a school which offers

French Immersion. There are no schools that offer this programme in the neighbourhood (indeed, French Immersion programmes have traditionally tended to be offered in affluent neighbourhoods in Western Canada) and school boards are required to provide bus transportation for students who attend French Immersion schools outside their school zone. I discussed this reality with Elaine, the school principal, in the following conversation:

Elaine: Anyways, the other thing within this area is we do lose some families to immersion because kids are then bussed out
Andrea: That's a solution out eh? Because they have the right to be
Elaine: And they do get transportation for that and so and on this side it's James Murray [French Immersion school] and I know we have kids within the general community who are bussed there

It is not only at the elementary school level that settler parents choose to have their children leave the neighbourhood to attend school in whiter spaces. During a conversation with Phoenix, who lives directly across the school, she explained to me that her oldest brother drives to a high school on the East Side. I mentioned this reality to Elaine in the following conversation:

Andrea: And at the high school level, do they have the choice to go where they want?
Elaine: At the high school level, they can go wherever they want, um, they basically, they're responsible for their transportation, there's subsidy bus tickets but ...
Andrea: Phoenix was telling me, and they live across the street, her brother drives to Laurier High everyday
Elaine: Hm-hmm, yeah, go figure and as much as possible I think the system has tried to balance programs east and west so there is an advanced component at Highland Mill so there's the tech programs at Victoria Road as well as at Laurier High

Highland Mill and Victoria Road, the two high schools mentioned by Elaine, are within 5–10 min driving distance from Phoenix's home. Yet, Phoenix's brother attends Laurier High, an East Side high school located roughly 20 min away by car.

While I suspect that there is more involved in these decisions than simply a desire for a better school, parental decisions regarding schools and French Immersion programmes could be justified by describing these choices as the best options for their children. It is my sense, however, that these decisions also reflect deliberate decisions to minimize contact between white settler children and Indigenous educators and students. While the previous excerpt describes situations with blurred undertones of racism, the following conversation describes situations where parents' choices of schools reflect their discomfort with First Nations educators and their view of schools as legitimate and, therefore, necessarily white spaces.

Elaine: When we talked about what would you do or would you do anything if parents were, I guess, when you knew that they were being racist in the sense that that they handled the teacher, and uh we lost two families last year and one in kindergarten and that one was, both cases, were about the teacher and they had an issue and couldn't get them, they didn't have a real curricular issue at all, but in their minds, they just, it was all about the teacher and you knew it wasn't the teacher, you knew it was about the person and there would certainly be a smaller First Nations population [at that school]

Andrea: Yeah, when I looked at the demographics, there were no First Nations, well according to self-identifying, there were no First Nations homes in that area really [the Catholic school-neighbourhood south of the neighbourhood]

Elaine: And I'm guessing there would be a few now but minimally and again in a different economic bracket so which makes some difference so we lost a couple families there and I mean, they did say the teacher, and one had a discussion with the superintendent and again, you provide the support here and bottom line, you have a great teacher, this isn't about the teacher and with the one, I had a phone call and I identified what it was about but you know, I guess my next thought, it's interesting to watch as our population, our Aboriginal population is increasing, in my mind, here in Saskatchewan what would be nice is if you get the kids being able to be comfortable with each other and to some extent, that happens here but, as you pointed out, to some extent in that classroom, there's a group and we have families that we draw from in Hillridge that should be going to Vincent Brown and they don't go there because Vincent Brown is almost exclusively Aboriginal population so, yeah, it's almost dilemma how much do you do here to try and make everybody comfortable because in the long term, that's what you want

In the above conversation with Elaine, she reveals, albeit indirectly, that some parents resist having their children instructed by First Nations teachers to the point that they choose to remove their children and send them to the Catholic school south of the neighbourhood. This interview excerpt brings to mind Carol Schick's descriptions of pre-service teachers' responses to being taught by a First Nations professor:

> Yet there are those in the university whose identities – such as the representative Aboriginal professor – who are perceived as being 'out of place.' Her embodied presence poses a dilemma for many of the participants; some of their greatest hostility is reserved for her. For, if she can be a legitimate authority in this site, and if participants' own legitimacy is dependent on their whiteness, the presence of the Aboriginal female professor undermines their entitlement. (Schick, 2002: 113)

For the resistant settler parents in the principal's anecdote, the presence of First Nations and Métis educators at this school undermines the entitlement of their children. If these teachers can be legitimate authorities in the white space of the school, the whiteness of their children ceases to matter. Whiteness, and the privilege it produces, is to be protected at all costs, including calls to principals and superintendents, hostile behaviour towards First Nations and Métis educators, and even withdrawing children from the school so that they can attend a school where whiteness is maintained.

Another incident that occurred outside the classroom also highlights the relationship between race, teachers as legitimate authorities, and white settlers' dependency on white educators for affirmation of their own legitimacy. As part of a unit on community, I accompanied Deborah and the students to a local hospital to attend a play. While at the hospital, Deborah addressed the students as a group, the children directed their questions to her, and Deborah directed me and the other educational assistant in our interactions with the students. Yet, even with all these indicators, hospital staff members still sought me out as the classroom teacher. I twice had to explain to white settler hospital staff that I was not the classroom teacher and point them in the direction of Deborah. In both cases, the individuals could not mask the surprise on their faces when discovering that they had mistaken me for the classroom teacher. I attribute their surprise, and subsequently their embarrassment, to our shared understanding that they overlooked Deborah as the classroom teacher because she is First Nations and, therefore, could not be a legitimate authority figure. Given the defined roles Deborah (teacher) and I (assistant) performed during the visit, it was interesting to see how deeply entrenched this understanding of white settler identity as authority can be.

Literacy as 'White Property'

During my time in the classroom, I observed Deborah's role as the classroom teacher being undermined by white settler parents on two occasions. These examples are related to the notion of literacy as white property (Prendergast, 2003) as well as idea of race-pleasure, that is, the pleasure involved in experiencing oneself as white through the process of noticing the Other (Farley, 1997). The situation in question originated, on the surface, from some English Language Arts worksheets completed by Devon, a white settler child. These worksheets were corrected by one of the white settler educational assistants in the classroom. Devon made several grammatical errors that the white settler educational assistant failed to notice and mistakenly marked as correct. The students' worksheets were sent home with all students to give to their parents. Early one Thursday morning in February, Deborah was called to the office. Devon's mother had noticed the correction mistakes and instead of raising her concerns with Deborah, she circled the mistakes, added sarcastic comments questioning first whether the rules of the English language had somehow changed and, at a second mistake, wrote 'you've got to be kidding me.' She then went directly to Elaine, the school principal, with the worksheets in hand as 'proof'.

In her typically direct and fair manner, Elaine supported Deborah and advised the parent to discuss the issue with the classroom teacher and apprised Deborah of the parent's complaint. I saw these particular worksheets; some of the parent's complaints were valid and in some places the parent was mistaken in her belief that something should have been marked as incorrect. Deborah was understandably upset by the parent's actions but her main issue was not that the parent had concerns about the correction of the homework but, rather, that the parent had not contacted her directly. Devon's mother bypassed discussions with the First Nations educator, the illegitimate authority in the classroom to whom 'standard' English and literacy did not belong, to address her concerns and point out Deborah's 'mistakes' to the white settler school principal. This questioning of Deborah's authority as a language arts teacher brings to mind the work of Nuzhat Amin (1999) on the stereotype of 'authentic ESL teacher'. Amin's study of the views of adult ESL (English as a second language) students in Canada found that some ESL students make two major assumptions: 'The first is that only White people can be native speakers of English and the second is that only native speakers know "real", "proper", "Canadian" English' (Amin, 1999: 94). In speaking of native and non-native speakers of English as teachers of TESOL, Shondel Nero (2006a) also links race to the legitimacy of English speakers when she suggests that 'the "nativeness" of most non-White speakers of English is often questioned' (Nero, 2006a: 29). Like the participants in Amin's study, Devon's mother was not prepared to accept Deborah as an authority on 'proper' English.

Over the next several weeks, a similar issue with worksheet corrections arose with the same parent and with another white settler parent in the classroom. This involvement of a second parent leads me to believe that these two parents had begun to discuss Deborah and her ability to evaluate English Language Arts assignments. Deborah chose to address the issue by first phoning both parents to apologize (never once explaining that the sheets had actually been corrected by an educational assistant and not by Deborah). Second, Deborah began personally correcting all the worksheets produced by the two white settler children in question as well as two others whom Deborah knew to be friendly with these mothers. In addition to her multiple tasks as a classroom teacher, Deborah also had to once again spend time and energy 'protecting' herself from the criticism and linguistic othering of white settler parents. She had to strategically counter the hostility of the white settler parents and defend her presence in this white space.

These incidents, and Elaine's comments regarding parents pulling their children from classrooms with First Nations teachers, led me to ask Deborah and other educators about how white settler parents treat First Nations educators in the school. In the following discussion, Corrine describes how some white settler parents interact with Deborah; other First Nations educators; and another instance of a white settler parent objecting to Indigenous content in one of the classes:

Andrea: Have you seen white parents treat Deborah differently?

Corrine: I would tend to agree that that would happen, yeah, yeah, I mean I've seen parents treat her differently because she's a female um, so yeah, there's definitely that in this neighbourhood, there's most definitely that in this neighbourhood, racism, in this neighbourhood, I mean we've had, last year we had a parent come in, nice skinhead-looking guy too, with sunglasses on his head and were just going to do teepee raising in the library, well he came he was just like, no way, and it wasn't even an Aboriginal teacher, it was a white teacher but I mean there was an Aboriginal woman coming in to show them about a tepee and what the poles mean and represent and whatever and this guy was adamant that no way are my kids taking any kind of Aboriginal education. Like, okay, but I mean he comes to the door, like a skinhead, shaved head, sunglasses and just like

Andrea: Did the children hear him say this?
Corrine: He was out in the hall but I mean yeah, no the kids didn't hear him but I mean, just very racist you know and I know there's been other parents in here with issues with Aboriginal teachers in the school. Yeah, I think that's why there are some parents that are harder on Deborah than they were on the previous teacher because the previous teacher is very white but she has low expectations for them. I mean I respect Deborah way more than any teacher I've worked with, she's an amazing teacher, she is very good with them and it boggles my mind that people can pick on her just because she's Aboriginal or because she's female, it's like, okay whatever, I mean she's got two strikes against her with some parents, she's a female and Aboriginal, they cannot see past it and see that's she's an awesome teacher. They don't ask the kids they just, it's amazing

Having heard Corrine's descriptions of some of the white settler parents' interaction with First Nations teachers and of their objections regarding inclusion of First Nations content in subject areas, I wondered how this might affect Deborah's experiences in the school. In the following exchange, I ask her about interaction with parents:

Deborah: I am, totally, and absolutely comfortable involving anything involving my First Nations and Métis students whereas with the others, I find that there's an invisible kind of barrier that I really can't go beyond
Andrea: Like you need to be careful with them?
Deborah: I need to be careful
Andrea: And why do you feel that, because of the kids' response or the parents?
Deborah: I guess, I don't know, maybe it's a personal, maybe not myself personally but I think it's something that, all those of us who are First Nations and teachers are still learning to work through and I guess that has to go back down to equality and uh and the question of whether the parents of these children actually recognize us as being...as being as capable as a white teacher, I guess, so I find that yeah, I don't teach them differently but when it comes to dealing with issues of personal nature, then I do, whereas with the First Nations children, I would never hesitate to call, never hesitate to drop in on a parent and because they're so much more open, no criticism

Deborah's use of 'invisible barrier' to explain her experiences with resistant white settler parents points to the racially spatialized reality of schools. This 'invisible barrier' functions as a way for white settlers to distance them from the illegitimate presence of Deborah and to maintain their and their children's own entitlement. The presence of Indigenous peoples and Indigenous knowledge in this white space threatens white settler entitlement. Maintaining 'invisible barriers' by: refusing to have children taught by First Nations teachers; moving children to other schools where the number of First Nations and Métis educators and students are fewer; questioning First Nations teachers' abilities to teach English Language Arts; and bypassing First Nations classroom teachers to address classroom concerns with administrator are all strategies of resistance/resentment employed by parents to protect their children's whiteness (as well as their own). It is also important to consider how this adult behaviour influences student behaviour both in terms of their relationships as well as their racialized identities. Beyond protecting the whiteness of spaces, parental resistance also potentially serves the purpose of socializing settler children into their own burgeoning performances of whiteness.

Not surprisingly, children in the school seem influenced by adult behaviour and comments; this reality was reflected in a number of my interviews with adult educators and students as well as my observations in classrooms and on the playground. I think these students are affected by what they learn or do not learn through curriculum; who they see as a legitimate authority in schools; and what they observe in terms of 'good' and 'bad' students in their classrooms. These messages cannot possibly go ignored by students nor do I think that white settler children have the types of critical literacy skills necessary to recognize and resist the colonialist discourses that circulate in society, in their homes, or at their schools. These colonialist discourses, like the ones I encountered as a child, serve to exalt white settler children and to protect our whiteness as legitimate. Consider the following example shared with me by Deborah during an interview. A Grade 2 child, not in the class that I observed, realized that Deborah was First Nations and loudly exclaimed to her classmates 'You're an Indian? Wait until I tell my mom!' This example and the previous interview reveal some of the ways in which racialized spaces become normalized for children.

It is important to note that I never observed any instances of students treating Deborah with disrespect. In fact, all of Deborah's students appeared to adore her, trust her completely and worked hard to please and to be close to her. My next area of discussion stems, rather, from the divide between Indigenous and white settler female students in Deborah's class and from one of the white settler male student's growing disdain for his school. The

Indigenous and white settler female students in the classroom where I conducted my research generally operate as separate friendship circles. With the exception of two girls (one First Nations and one white settler) who live next door to one another, the two groups of girls do not mix. When given the choice during classroom activities, the white settler girls work with the white settler girls and the First Nations girls remain together as well. The same behaviours occur on the playground as well as outside the school (based on what the children shared with me about their out-of-school experiences).

I spoke with Deborah about my observation early on in my study. She explained to me that Crystal, a First Nations student, had attempted to befriend Hannah and Jessica, two white settler girls, early on in the school year. Deborah explained that Crystal's overtures of friendship had been rejected. In discussion with me, Deborah described Crystal as 'too much, too pushy' for Hannah and pointed out the differences in the girls' backgrounds: Hannah was from a white middle-class background and Crystal was Cree and moved back and forth between her First Nation and the city. Crystal's failed attempts at friendship culminated in Hannah leaving school for a week because her parents felt that she was being 'intimidated by Crystal.' Hannah was never able to verbalize what Crystal was actually doing to her, but since that moment, Deborah explained that the two groups of girls simply did not mix. Deborah also explained that this occurrence of separate friendship groups was not an anomaly in terms of what she had observed throughout her years teaching at this school. In the following excerpt from an interview with Hannah, I attempt to discuss with her why she does not play with Crystal, Chantelle, Amber, Starr and two other First Nations girls:

Andrea: But would your mom let you play with them if you wanted to?
Hannah: Hmm, no
Andrea: Why?
Hannah: I just never play with them, I don't know why, I don't really, like I notice them, but I don't really play with them because they're not really my friends because um, they don't like me and I don't like them
Andrea: Do you think that they don't like you?
Hannah: Well they don't
Andrea: Well I don't know, I see Crystal over there sometimes trying to hang out with you and Jessica
Hannah: Hmmm
Andrea: You've never noticed that?
Hannah: Hmm

While Hannah is not able to name her reasons for not playing with Crystal or the other First Nations girls, she does seem aware that she is not friends with them. I do not wish to sensationalize the words or behaviour of this young girl or imply that there is conscious malevolence or racism in her decision not to play with her First Nations peers. There is something familiar, though, about her indifference towards the First Nations girls in her classroom. I want to use this instance of two friendship circles not mixing to draw attention to the settler tradition of 'indifference' towards First Nations women. Take, for example, Sherene Razack's descriptions of the disappearance of three First Nations women in Saskatchewan in the early 1990s at the hands of a white man name John Crawford. Razack writes that 'the women's disappearance attracted little attention. When their families reported them missing, police appeared to assume that such women were simply transients on the move' (Razack, 2002: 135). Learning indifference towards Indigenous women (and to fear First Nations men), at least until they enter into spaces where they are not supposed to, for example as teachers in settler schools, is likely something that settler children learn at a very young age. As such, while I stated earlier that I do not wish to sensationalize the friendship choices that Hannah makes, I also do not wish to dismiss them as inconsequential.

The other event that I would like to discuss in this section relates to Devon, a white settler male student. In January 2006, the school where I was conducting my study experienced 'lockdown' because of a child who brought a realistic-looking toy gun to school. As I understand it, someone saw the toy, told a teacher and the RCMP were called in to investigate. The lockdown lasted roughly an hour and then classes resumed regularly. As a result of the event the school received media coverage that day; indeed, when Deborah asked me to pull the blinds at the beginning of the lockdown, media vehicles were already parked outside. Aware that parents needed to be updated on the events of the day, each child was given a note from the school principal to take home with them at the end of the day.

Devon was very troubled by the lockdown that day and understandably so. It seemed to take a number of weeks for him to settle into classroom routines and to feel comfortable when the classroom lights were turned out or the classroom door was closed. I find these to be normal reactions to the events that occurred at the school. What I had problems with was the message Devon was receiving at home and, in turn, bringing to school with him. Devon's mother, one of the parents I discussed earlier who had had problems with Deborah's homework corrections, seemed to indicate to Devon that it was the [illegitimate] nature of his school that had caused the lockdown to occur. Devon began to tell his classmates that 'Community schools are bad' and pointed out that this type of event would not occur at his brother's school, another school (French Immersion) in the city. Incidentally, other staff members explained to me that there had been lockdowns at other city schools in the fall months of that school year. Sensitive to Devon's concerns, Deborah attempted to calm Devon by discussing his concerns and by explaining that these incidents could have occurred at another school. Nonetheless, Deborah's discussions with Devon did not seem to dissuade him of his beliefs regarding his school.

Beliefs and feelings are difficult patterns to isolate; one must make inferences based on the comments and behaviour of an individual. Based on the children's utterances in both situations described in the above section, I put forward the idea that Hannah has developed ambivalent feelings towards her First Nations female peers and that Devon is developing a negative opinion of his inner-city school community. It seems likely that some of this behaviour stems from ideas and behaviour modelled by their parents. The children's ideas demonstrate some of how the racial spatialization of Indigenous and white settler communities is perpetuated by the socialization of children into appropriate roles and positions of power, just as was the case for me as a young white settler child during the activities of my Grade 6 school year.

Conclusion

This chapter provides an exploration of the racialization of school spaces and the types of encounters that take place in these locations. My observations and the excerpts taken from interviews with children and adults add to the story about how racial hierarchies are created and maintained in settler societies. The racialization of space in this urban community is aided, in part, by the river that separates the city into East and West. Comments made by educators and children reveal the 'criminality' of the West Side; this space is poor, dangerous and the area where First Nations, Métis and working class white settlers *choose* to live. In contrast, the East side with the respectability of its settler families is thought to be safe, affluent and the domain of a mainly middle-class white settler population.

The racialization of space as discussed in this chapter is, in part, maintained by white settler resistance to First Nations and Métis' encroachment on the official white spaces of schools. White settler parents use a number of approaches to avoid sending their children to schools with high Indigenous populations or where their child may potentially be instructed by a First Nations teacher. Additionally, these parental strategies affect the teaching experiences of First Nations educators and their relationships with white settler parents and children. Finally, it would seem that white settler parents' behaviour influences the beliefs and behaviours of their children, thus further perpetuating the cycle of division. It is only by resurrecting the historical memory of colonization, as I have aimed to do in this book, that we might contest the practices of domination that continue to create racialized spaces such as the inner city, suburbs and the settler school.

6 Suppressing Linguistic Alterity in Settler Schools

Linguistic Dominance

Discussions of language standards and prescriptivism are never straightforward (Bex & Watts, 1999; Honey, 1997; Trudgill, 1998). Such debates address divergent themes ranging from providing access to power through standard languages, to the necessity of written norms, to the suitability of one variety (British) over another (American) to serve as this norm and to the role of schools in promoting 'standard' varieties to the exclusion of other varieties. The movements we now call imperialism and colonialism have implications both in terms of the emergence of new English varieties (and other colonial languages) through colonial contact as well as in terms of linguistic dominance. European imperialism led to the creation of new varieties of colonial languages through sustained contact between colonizers, settlers and Indigenous peoples (Kachru, 1992; Mesthrie & Bhatt, 2008; Nero, 2006a). Scholarly dialogue has devoted itself to discussing both *the ways* in which English has moved around the planet as the result of imperial, colonial and global processes as well as *the consequences* of its diffusion to a variety of locations (Canagarajah, 1999; Clemente & Higgins, 2008; Pavlenko, 2002; Pennycook, 1998, 2003; Makoni & Pennycook, 2007; Sharifian, 2009). And while one of the effects of British imperialism was the introduction of English to other areas of the world, the English(es) heard in places ranging from Canada to Hong Kong is decidedly heterogeneous. The English language is increasingly diverse; it has becomes a network of interrelated Englishes, each of which is influenced by factors such geographic location, cultures and other languages (Lo Bianco, 2000).

While the global processes discussed in this chapter created linguistic diversity in terms of the emergence of these new versions of colonial languages, it has also created linguistic adversity. Within the former colonies of the former British empire, not all English language varieties are considered equal and, in many cases, performances of English that deviate from 'standard' norms are seen as nothing more than linguistic aberrances. However, this reality is not actually related to linguistic structures or the greater suitability of one language to express an argument over another. The positioning of one language variety over another is directly linked to that nation's colonial past and, as Bourdieu explains, the official language variety and its role as 'the theoretical norm against which all linguistic practices are objectively measured' (Bourdieu, 1991: 45). As such, the settler variety of English that I speak in the Canadian province of Saskatchewan, for example, is considered preferable in settler schools to the varieties of English spoken by Indigenous peoples in my province (Heit & Blair, 1993; Sterzuk, 2008).

As discussed in Chapter 2, postcolonial thinking tells us that Cartesian philosophy and European imperialism continue to have implications in the world in many ways including a particular Western worldview that accompanied European expansion. In settler societies, this view of the world and the settler self's place in it includes the settler Self's fear of the Indigenous Other's alterity; the settler goal of bringing 'knowledge' to the Indigenous other under the guise of 'development'; the settler Self's need to suppress alterity through the promotion of homogeneity; and heterogeneous settler populations united in the shared goal of gaining control over Indigenous peoples. From this perspective, then, language education which seeks to promote one 'Standard' English over others; negates indigenized English varieties; and positions Indigenous students as less capable of developing reading literacy is a product of settler nationalist ideologies which contributes to the reproduction of the racial hierarchy of white settler colonies.

The bias towards settler varieties of English and the struggles this creates for many Indigenous students in settler schools in Canada (Genee, 2010; Heit & Blair, 1993; Sterzuk, 2008; Wiltse, 2008) shares similarities with the struggles for legitimacy of speakers of hybridized varieties of colonial languages in other settler societies: speakers of African American Englishes in the United States (Baugh, 1983; Green, 2002; Labov, 1972; Lee, 2006; Mufwene *et al.*, 1998; Prendergast, 2003; Rickford, 1999; Smitherman, 1977); speakers of Aboriginal Englishes in Australia (Arthur, 1996; Malcolm, 1995, 2001; Malcolm & Sharifian, 2004; Sharifian, 2001, 2006, 2008; Sharifian *et al.*, 2004); speakers of Indigenous Spanishes in Mexico (Flores Farfán, 1999); speakers of Caribbean Creole Englishes in the Caribbean (Nero, 2006a; Pratt-Johnson, 2006; Winer, 2006); speakers of Hawai'in Creole in Hawai'i (Eades *et al.*, 2006; Sakoda & Siegel, 2003); and for the Kashinawa-influenced Portuguese of the Kashinawa peoples in the western Amazon region of Brazil and Peru (Menezes de Souza, 2002). There are clearly differences between the local contexts of these language varieties and the degrees to which they are similar to and vary from official language varieties. What the stories of speakers of these language varieties share in common is a colonial past which shapes the present and the struggle to have their literacy practices and language varieties recognized as legitimate by settler schools.

This book is concerned with colonialist ideologies and the deficit discourses about the linguistic deficiencies of Indigenous students in settler schools. Despite differences between individuals, many practices in settler schools continue to produce inequity through the privileging of 'standard' language and the linguistic othering of Indigenous students (and Others). Deficit discourses about indigenized varieties of colonial languages continue to circulate in settler schools (Nero, 2006a). Such discourses include messages about 'proper' forms of language and produce indigenized varieties as incomplete or inaccurate versions of legitimate settler varieties.

Educational research links teacher expectations of students who are speakers of English language varieties not sanctioned by schools to lower levels of literacy development as well as academic failure (see Delpit & Dowdy, 2002; Labov, 1972; Lee, 2006; Malcolm, 1995, 2001; Mufwene et al., 1998; Nero, 2006a; Prendergast, 2003; Rickford, 1999; Sterzuk, 2009a; Wolfram et al., 1999). Standard language views of English – or socially constructed views about languages, in terms of how, where, when and with whom they should and should not be spoken and written – have many implications for education. These types of views about what constitutes legitimate language, particularly when held by educational gatekeepers such as administrators, curriculum designers, teachers and speech and language pathologists, can negatively impact speakers of 'illegitimate' languages and language varieties (Bourdieu, 1991).

In schools, English language variation can often be viewed as a detriment, as something that gets in the way of acquiring literacy skills and mastering subject material (Nero, 2006b). Biased language beliefs legitimatize discriminatory school practices, and traditional teaching practices in culturally and linguistically diverse classrooms can consign linguistically and culturally diverse students to failure and to the 'perception that they are intellectually incompetent' (Cohen & Lotan, 2004: 736). None of this research claims that teaching 'standard English' writing is wrong or unnecessary. Educational researchers generally support the position that schools need to provide all students with access to language varieties and literacy practices that have been deemed as legitimate by society and societal institutions (Delpit, 1988). This scholarly literature does maintain, rather, that when teachers view English language variation as evidence of deficiency or delays in language development and, therefore erroneously believe such students to be less capable of developing print literacy skills, then it is necessary to examine the nature of teacher views of language.

This book argues that standard language discourses are evidence of colonialist and nationalist ideologies about 'standard language' and these messages circulate in schools and society through curricular documents, academic publications and teacher education programmes. And just like the idea of *terra nullius*, these ideas are deeply rooted in many societies and we are often unaware of their origins. Understanding how the acceptance of some varieties as 'standard' became common sense better positions us to be able to de-naturalize our thinking around language standards.

Standard Language Cultures

Sociolinguist James Milroy describes ideologies about standard language and the effects of such views in the following way:

> Certain languages, including widely used ones such as English, French, and Spanish, are believed by their speakers to exist in standardized forms, and this kind of belief affects the way in which speakers think about their own language and about 'language' in general. We may say that speakers of these languages live in **standard language cultures**. (Milroy, 2001: 531, emphasis in the original).

Milroy's statement is significant for a couple of reasons. First, he acknowledges the socially constructed nature of such views on standardized forms of languages. The 'naturalness' of standard forms of languages is not universal; not all language communities view languages in this way. Milroy's statement is also important because it highlights the cultural aspect of this particular ideology. Using this idea, we can say that settler societies, like the ones described in this book, are standard language cultures. In such cultures, 'the standard language' is legitimate and other varieties are rendered illegitimate.

Whereas other types of bias and discrimination are often attributed to small-minded or unenlightened people, standard language discourses seem to be taken up by all facets of such a society. In the foreword to Shondell Nero's 2006 edited volume on English language variation and education, Peter Elbow explains the prevalence of these types of beliefs in the following statement:

> Language prejudice runs startlingly deep – in some ways deeper than racial prejudice. When I encounter tolerant people who are remarkable for their openness to dangerous ideas and wrong practices that mainstream society rejects – people who above all sincerely reject racism – I find that

a good number of them are deeply intolerant of language they call wrong or bad. They welcome all people and ideas – as long as they are 'well spoken'. (Elbow, 2006: ix)

I have met these people too. What we can ascertain from the prevalence and acceptability of such beliefs in standard language cultures is that such discourses experience high traffic throughout standard language cultures and that we have not become adept at (a) recognizing these discourses or (b) introducing alternative discourses. This lack of response might be related to the privilege afforded to speakers of 'standard' languages and to the idea that such varieties are available to anyone if only they have the desire and motivation to acquire them. With enough 'pioneer grit' anyone can learn to 'speak proper English'.

So, what kind of processes creates 'standard language' and what kind of discourses circulate in standard language cultures? To answer this question, let us begin by examining the role of print-capitalism in first naturalizing the idea of 'standard' languages. Benedict Anderson explains that the 16th century was a time of 'exceptional European prosperity' (Anderson, 1983: 38) and that book publishers shared in the economic successes of this time. Book-sellers first focused on Latin-readers and after they saturated this market, they targeted the 'potentially huge markets' of the vernacular masses: languages such as French, Spanish and Italian. Targeting these markets meant that language standardization became necessary because:

> In pre-print Europe, and, of course, elsewhere in the world, the diversity of spoken languages, those languages that for their speakers were (and are) the warp and woof of their lives, was immense; so immense, indeed, that had print-capitalism sought to exploit each potential oral vernacular market, it would have remained a capitalism of petty proportions. But these varied idiolects were capable of being assembled, within definite limits, into print-languages far fewer in number ... Nothing served to 'assemble' related vernaculars more than capitalism, which within the limits imposed by grammars (and syntaxes, created mechanically reproduced print-languages capable of dissemination through the market. (Anderson, 1983: 41)

Print-capitalism provided 'the bases for national consciousness in three distinct ways' (Anderson, 1983: 41). First, book publishers established 'unified fields of exchange' for speakers of 'the huge variety of Frenches, Englishes, or Spanishes' (Anderson, 1983: 42). These speakers were then able to understand one another through print. Through this comprehension, people become aware of the language groups to which they belonged. Anderson argues that this awareness 'formed the embryo of the nationally imagined community' (Anderson, 1983: 42). A shared sense of a standard language implied belonging to a national community. Print-capitalism also provided a 'new fixity to language, which in the long run helped to build that image of antiquity so central to the subjective idea of the nation' (Anderson, 1983: 42). Finally, print-capitalism created languages of power; certain varieties were closer to print-languages, and this, in turn, created a subordinate status for those varieties that were not close to the print-languages. Print-capitalism laid the groundwork for national consciousness, created unified and fixed fields of exchanges and gave status and prestige to particular varieties. The final point is central to the discussion in this chapter.

The establishment of 'definite limits' for languages had little in common with the planned language policies of today or the ideologies of standard languages as 'natural' that I speak about in this book. Indeed, Anderson describes the standardization that emerged out of print-capitalism process as 'unconscious' but indicates that once these 'standards' were established, they became 'formal models to be imitated' (Anderson, 1983: 42). Standardization or the imposition of uniformity on particular 'class of objects' (Milroy, 2001: 531) such as language (Milroy, 2001) was not in and of itself the product of ideologies, as we can see in Anderson's discussion of print-capitalism. And yet, because of their function as 'formal models to be imitated,' these varieties have 'been equated with the "highest prestige variety", rather than with the variety that is characterized by the highest degree of uniformity' (Milroy, 2001: 532). Language varieties acquire prestige not through high levels of uniformity but when 'their speakers have high prestige' (Milroy, 2001: 532). Stop for a moment and consider which speakers of English have the highest prestige in a settler society created as an overseas replica of British society and as a racial hierarchy.

While linguists may acknowledge that no one variety is more 'standard' than other; people who live in standard language cultures tend to believe otherwise. As constructed as these views on language are, the 'formal models' that we are taught to imitate and emulate circulate throughout settler schools and other official spaces. Recognizing that how ideologies and discourses work to produce societal structures is important. In addition to a popular belief in the naturalness of standardized languages, Milroy also articulates a number of popular attitudes found in standard language culture. One such aspect is a 'firm belief in correctness' (Milroy, 2001: 535). This particular cultural aspect is particularly relevant in this book's discussion of linguistic prescriptivism in schools. Correctness as a belief dictates that 'when there are two or more variants of some word or construction, only one of them can be right. The correctness of one particular form is taken for granted; it is common sense and "no justification is needed for rejecting" it' (Milroy, 2001: 535). Milroy explains that these common-sense views towards correctness are 'ideologically loaded attitudes' but that people who hold them do not see their positions in this way: they believe that:

> Their adverse judgements on persons who use language 'incorrectly' are purely linguistic judgements sanctioned by authorities on language, and this belief is itself partly a consequence of standardization. People do not necessarily associate these judgements with prejudice or discrimination in terms of race or social class: they believe that, whatever the social characteristics of the speakers may be, these people have simply used the language in an erroneous way and that it is up to them to learn to speak correctly. If they do not do this, it is their own fault as individuals, whatever their race, color, creed or class: there are plenty of models for them of 'good' speech. (Milroy, 2001: 536)

The white settler and First Nations and Métis educators involved in this study discussed awareness of language variation in terms of potential differences between Englishes spoken by First Nations and Métis peoples and by white settlers. While awareness of linguistic and discourse differences is apparent, this consciousness does not necessarily extend to an understanding of Indigenous English as a legitimate English variety. Eller (1989) suggests that viewing a minority language variety as substandard is the evidence of educator bias. She also maintains that the tendency to label children as verbally inept is a result of the majority's need for these children to conform to their own linguistic models. None of the educators with whom I spoke in the school had any awareness of ideas such as language variation; the hybridity of languages; or of Indigenous English as a legitimate language variety. Instead, I found educators with a 'firm belief in correctness' who openly discussed the 'deficit' in First Nations and Métis students' language. Alternately, I also found educators who, while not familiar with the idea of language variation, were open to my descriptions of Indigenous English as a legitimate variety of English.

There is a potential moment of moral judgement that occurs when a 'mistake' is made in the production of language. Not being able to recognize a language 'mistake' means that 'if individuals do not know this kind of thing, they identify themselves as not belonging to the community that can distinguish right from wrong' (Milroy, 2001: 537). I think it is possible to take Milroy's argument one step further and examine the discursive production of race that occurs in moments when a speaker of a settler variety of a language judges a speaker of an indigenized variety as unable to distinguish linguistic right from wrong, as evidenced by their failure to follow the model of 'good speech' that is readily available to them. The power to correct or know better than the linguistic deviant reaffirms the settler's position as a legitimate speaker of the colonial language. In settler societies, there exists the assumption that 'correct' linguistic models are available to Indigenous students if they would only avail themselves of what schools offer. For many, their failure to do so establishes them as unable to distinguish between right and wrong; they are once again linked to criminality. Consider the following excerpt from my interview with Lisa, a white settler educator in my study:

Andrea: Okay, is there anything that you'd like to add that we haven't already talked about or anything that you just want to mention?

Lisa: I, just uh, the importance of early language because we're feeling the deficits when they get up to grade 2 or 3. They just can't write a proper sentence because they can't speak, they don't speak with complete sentences, or they don't, we can't really anticipate what word would come next because they don't really use proper grammar necessarily and, uh, 'how do you spell gonna,' well it's 'going to.' 'How do you spell grewed, growed?' Well, so it's just a lot.

Similarly, Anita also attributes academic difficulties of First Nations students to concerns over their 'language levels'. In the following utterance, Anita answers a question about factors that possibly contribute to higher rates of *retention*, or the decision to hold a child back from advancing to the next grade, among Indigenous students than among white settler children in the school. Anita provides the following explanation for these higher rates of retention among First Nations and Métis students:

Anita: I think that, again, (higher levels of retention among First Nations and Métis children) is because of difference in level of language skills because they do present very different levels, in the past, here, we don't usually retain kids anymore, they, um, I probably have it somewhere if you want, the research done, retaining does not improve anything

Anita and Lisa's statements reveal a belief in the prevalence of lower language skills among Indigenous students. While it is possible that some students may have delays, it is not likely that this is a characteristic common to all Indigenous students. Instead, it is more likely that language assessments tools are not linguistically and culturally appropriate for speakers of Indigenous English and teaching methods used are not effective for students who do not speak settler varieties of English. Also interesting is Anita's statement regarding the retention of students. She was not the only educator to inform me of the school policy against retention, yet I found evidence of student retention in conversations with children and educators as well in official school records of students.

The following two educator comments contain views of language that differ from the above descriptions of Indigenous English as evidence of a language deficit. The first excerpt is from an interview with Tom who is a Métis educator at the school:

Tom: So if we're trying to encourage these children to speak but every time, you know, they're saying something improperly because it doesn't flow with that certain type of sentence structure that we're expecting. You're closing that bridge um and you're not going to have that language development with that child. You're just going to see deficit because every time you set them down for testing, well, they have presented with that opportunity to grow, when you work with elders and stuff, and they're working with children, you'll see that constant interaction with them. And, again, that is broken when we get here, um, you know, when it's time for adults to speak, kind of thing, is when kids are meant not to be heard, they're just supposed to sit there and listen. But during traditional teachings there will be that constant interaction with the elders, with the kids, and nobody's going to sit back and the elder's not going to criticize a kid for not speaking properly, because it's not as important as the kid being able to learn, you know, from the story. If you're following me ...

In his comments, Tom explains that, from his perspective, focusing on learning is more important than being concerned with what might be perceived as proper grammar by some educators. Other First Nations educators at the school made similar comments about language. While they did not use terms such as *language variety* or even *dialect* or describe Indigenous English as rule governed, they did talk about it simply being the way people speak in their communities. Print literacy development was highly valued by these First Nations and Métis educators but they did not perceive 'not speaking properly' as the largest stumbling block to a child's progress in school.

Similar to Tom's comments, the following statement made by white settler educator Rachel demonstrates awareness and acceptance of the variety of English spoken by her Indigenous students:

Rachel: I point that out all the time and I don't penalize them for it, when they speak like that. We're writing essays right now and I was just talking about this with somebody the other day because I was stuck between, I know that's the way she speaks and I know that's the way they speak at home and that's the way they speak on the reserve and great. And so, when I talk to her about her essay, I said, in formal writing, for example, if you went beyond elementary school and into high school and college and you were writing a formal essay, you would be asked to change these words. And it should look like this. And then I said, in speaking, speak however you want to speak but recognize that when we're writing the essay it needs to look like this. Just like, when you're doing a title page, and that's the example I used, when you're doing a title page for your short stories, put pictures all over it, any font you want but when you're doing a title page for your essay, it's in Arial 12 font and we do it like this. Was that right or wrong?

Rachel's comments demonstrate an acceptance of Indigenous English as her students' language variety. Yet, she also understands that her students require explicit instruction in norms of written English and seems to be intuitively using a contrastive analysis approach in teaching written norms of language (Rickford, 2006), as discussed in Chapters 2 and 7. Finally, her final question indicates a desire to serve the best interests of her students and to modify her teaching approach if it is not effective in bridging her students' home and school languages.

Rachel's views of Indigenous English were unlike the other white settler educators interviewed in this study. She taught older grades, and so she was not involved in the early literacy education like some of the other white settler educators that I interviewed. This difference in the grade level might have had some influence on her decision to view her students' languages as full and appropriate. By 'full and appropriate', I mean that Rachel did not see her students' language as deficient or insufficient for their literacy-making purposes. In addition to the difference in grade level, Rachel's educational background and life experiences may also have influenced her views of her students' Englishes. Rachel majored in Native Studies during her undergraduate studies in education; these studies seemed to provide with a deeper sense of the ways in which colonialism continued to influence her students' lives.

Another probable influence on her views of language is the literacy organization she worked with while completing her undergraduate degree. This volunteer experience provided her with training and experience as a literacy tutor. During this volunteer experience, Rachel worked with a Métis woman. Rachel described their approach to tutoring writing in adolescent First Nations boys in the following way:

Rachel: I did a group with the boys and I worked with a Métis woman and we did the programme together and we talked before we went how we were going to be, we decided we just want these boys talking and writing and communicating with language without worrying about us coming down on them and she talked about language, 'it's their language'

It is also likely significant that Rachel grew up in a province outside the Canadian prairies and only moved to Saskatchewan in her late teens. Growing up away from the colonial and racist discourses which seem heightened in Saskatchewan might also play a role in her perceptions of legitimate language and her own racialized identity.

The interview excerpts discussed in this section demonstrate that educators are aware of Indigenous English. First Nations and Métis educators seem to have a more inclusive view of language in that they accept students' speech as culturally appropriate. Similarly, white settler educator Rachel demonstrates awareness of Indigenous English as a language variety particular to First Nations speech communities. As such, she understands the relationship between spoken English and developing written English abilities and adjusts her teaching accordingly. Alarmingly, a number of white settler educators do not share this more expansive view of language and attribute linguistic differences to the notion of language deficiency.

Literacy Development

When conducting literacy research in schools, it seems important to question power relations, discourses and the construction of student identities. Biased views of linguistic variation – when held by educational policy makers, administrators and educators – can affect the literacy, academic and social development of speakers of indigenized and othered English language varieties. The findings of the previous section demonstrate that some educators at my research site seem to have negative perceptions of Indigenous English. My biggest source of information regarding how literacy and reading programmes are structured in the school was Deborah, the classroom teacher with whom

I worked. I was able to see how she worked with the children and also gain insight into their literacy experiences in previous grades. I also learned that, of the approximately 25 students in her class, three (all First Nations) had been retained in earlier grades. In terms of speech and language assessment, seven children had been referred in earlier grades, only one was a white settler. While I did not conduct an empirical review of student retentions or of speech and language referrals, based on my interviews with children and adults; conversations; review of the cumulative files of the students in Deborah's classroom; and observations, I believe that First Nations and Métis children in this school experience these things more frequently than white settlers. Deborah, who has been teaching in the school for almost 10 years, as well as other educators in my study, supported this view.

Children in this school have their reading tested through the use of two standardized tests. These tests are used to assess whether a child is at grade level in reading and to determine areas of reading which are most difficult for a particular child. If a child scores below grade level early in the year, they are tested again in the winter months to ascertain if improvement has been made. During my time in Deborah's class, I was able to observe this second series of testing. Interestingly, on the first test, almost all the First Nations and Métis children were 1–2 years below grade level in their reading abilities. While one or two white settler students had some reading struggles, none of them were a full grade level behind the grade-level score. At the time of the second series of testing, conducted by Deborah and the resource room teacher, all the First Nations and Métis children had made improvements in their reading abilities to the point where some were at grade level and others were only considered to be a half year behind.

Deborah and I discussed the results of the First Nations and Métis students in her classroom. All had lower scores in the area of reading comprehension. Deborah explained that word recognition and oral reading did not appear to be challenges to them but they struggled with retelling stories and answering comprehension questions. That is to say that the children had the ability to decode language but did not appear to have developed strategies to achieve comprehension. What this seems to suggest is that these students previous experiences with reading likely targeted decoding skills – sounding words out, memorizing words, teaching the relationship between sounds and letters – which, when not combined with comprehension strategies, can result in students who can read but not make sense of what they are reading.

In contrast, Deborah teaches decoding skills (sometimes referred to as 'word attack' skills) and aims to improve her students' phonological awareness but also focuses on assisting her students in developing the comprehension strategies they can use to understand a text and scaffolds them in their comprehension. She teaches them to pay attention to titles and to examine pictures; she reminds them of previous experiences they might have had with their families that are similar to what they are reading about; she reviews potentially unfamiliar vocabulary; she stops reading to do comprehension checks; and she leads the children in a discussion of the text topic before, during and after reading. In short, she uses all possible means to 'front-load' the story and to trigger previous schemas in an effort to enable comprehension and so that comprehension strategies are modelled for and explained to her students. I asked Deborah about her ideas and goals behind the strategies she uses. She explained that a lot of the texts her students are expected to read are not culturally appropriate (not just in a traditional/western cultural sense but in terms of their urban inner-city realities). In light of this fact, she often chooses texts that are related to the lived experiences of her students. Deborah is also keenly aware that her students will not always be provided with culturally relevant material and, as such, wants them to have the skills to tackle any new reading material.

It seems likely that Deborah's students' gains in their scores on these tests are tied to her focus on teaching reading strategies. Additionally, like the white settler teacher Rachel discussed in the previous section, Deborah seems to have an awareness that her students need to be able to recognize differences between English language varieties. For example, on one occasion, I heard her ask the following to Crystal, 'Do we say *et*?' At this point, Crystal was able to erase *et* from her text and replace it with *ate*. I will discuss this particular approach in more depth in Chapter 7.

Deborah's classroom was a rich learning environment in the area of Language Arts. To better understand what was possibly happening in other classrooms that might help to explain Deborah's students' initial difficulties with reading comprehension, I asked questions to other educators at the school about their beliefs and practices related to literacy development. The following excerpt is from an interview with white settler educator Lisa whose class consists of 18 First Nations students and one white settler student:

Andrea: And have any of these children repeated kindergarten or grade 1?
Lisa: Let me, I always have to go through the class, one, two, three, four, five, five off the top of my head, this one is going to repeat this year, six, without checking their files I would say 6 out of 19 have repeated already
Andrea: And you say that that's mostly due to literacy development?

Lisa: Yeah, yeah, they come in, they have significant delays in all literacy areas, in speech patterns, articulation, vocabulary, um, listening skills, if you read a story, they just don't get it, they don't have the kind of background

Andrea: Hm-hmm, what kind of stories do you use?

Lisa: A lot of the early, who do I like, I like Dr Seuss for all the rhyming, I like Robert Munsch for the repetition, and they usually find his are funny, they most often can grasp that situation, anything more imaginative is tough, anything slightly removed from their world, which I find has been quite narrow, is tough. I'll read some Aboriginal stories and it's fun to see their eyes light up at something familiar, or we've made bannock or something like that, you can really see there's a link, but I find a lot of times, there aren't

Lisa's description of the literacy skills of her students seems to indicate lowered expectations of their literacy and language abilities, and little, if any, understanding of their language as legitimate. In a subsequent interview with Deborah, I asked her about how white settler educators in her school perceived the literacy development of First Nations and Métis students:

Deborah: (sigh) it's always like, they don't understand, the comprehension's not there, the vocabulary's not there, and it's always, the understanding's not there, they're not quick enough for recall, their attention, there's always...

Deborah's ability to accurately reproduce her colleagues' beliefs about First Nations and Métis students' language and literacy development points to these views as discourses in circulation throughout the school. My short time in the school left me with the impression that First Nations and Métis students are perceived, by many white settler educators, as arriving at school with limited language abilities.

As a result of these perceptions of their language abilities, First Nations and Métis students in this school do not appear to be expected to do well in developing literacy skills. This limited potential for literacy development seems to be attributed to the home environment. It is possible that First Nations and Métis students do have pre-school experience with literacy, language, speech and interaction that differ from the experiences of settler children. Indeed, there exists a substantial body of literature that examines the impact of differences between home and school in terms of experiences with literacy practices and culturally specific communication such as turn-taking and the use of silence (Cazden, 1988; Crago, 1992; Brice-Heath, 1983; Darnell, 1981; Delpit, 1995; Ferrara, 1999; Lee, 2006; Michaels, 1981; Plank, 1994; Scollon & Scollon, 1979, 1981, 1984). It has also been suggested that children who speak minority varieties of a language do not automatically become fluent in the school-sanctioned variety of a language upon entering school (Blake & Van Sickle, 2001; Roy, 1987). Many maintain that fluency of this kind can only be achieved through formal instruction and through explicit and direct explanations of the differences between the two varieties (Delpit, 1988; Rickford, 2006; Wolfram *et al.*, 1999). It has also been argued that lack of fluency in the variety valued by the school causes interruptions and delays in students' mastery of literacy skills and, subsequently, subject matter. A number of approaches have been suggested to help students in bridging between home and school varieties of language (Malcolm, 1995, 2001; Wolfram *et al.*, 1999).

Purcell-Gates (2002) argues that it is important for educators to understand limited experience with written language as a *difference* and not as a *deficit* as this distinction affects teacher expectations of learning. In the school described in this study, these children are not expected to do well in developing literacy skills and, often, the blame is placed on the home environment. Deborah made efforts to increase students' experiences with written language and the results seem to indicate improvement in their literacy skills. As outlined by Deyhle and Swisher (1997), deficit theories have been used to imply both biological and home environmental inadequacies in minority children, conveniently avoiding the examination of any role that schools might have in Indigenous students' academic difficulties.

Based on the interview data presented in this chapter, it seems clear that educator approaches need to be modified when working with children who speak indigenized (and othered) varieties of English. Teachers need to be more aware of language variation and how this affects literacy development and much work has to be done in terms of developing settler teachers' awareness of their own racialized identities and how this affects their views of their students' language and their potential for print literacy development. These pedagogical implications will be further discussed in the recommendations presented in Chapter 7.

Conclusion

This chapter has examined the imaginary linguistic homogeneity that settler schools promote through curriculum, testing and classroom activities. I have argued for a view of settler societies as linguistically heterogeneous places and hybridized varieties of English as natural phenomena in such spaces. Yet, despite the predictability of variation in language, many continue to equate speaking 'proper English' or English with one type of accent as a commitment to the nation or as part of development and progress. This nationalist view of language is one aspect of settler society efforts to produce a homogeneous population where none exists. This book seeks to problematize foundational fictions and myths of common destiny in order to disrupt the harmful practices and policies that accompany such nationalist ideologies.

As I have argued in this chapter, the notion of one language variety being more legitimate or official than another is a popular, but invented, aspect of standard language cultures. The view of language variation presented in this book derives from the understanding that 'languages are social inventions that have emerged in the discursive spaces of colonial and postcolonial times' (Clemente & Higgins, 2008: 22). Print-capitalism may have standardized languages for the sake of economic interests but these originally ideologically free views of 'correct' language have subsequently become ideologically laden with notions about right and wrong ways of speaking, writing and being. In settler societies, educator deficit discourses about language are not simply misunderstandings or conflicting views about how to communicate; they are fed by very old colonialist views of the Other.

I have argued that the discourses that circulate within settler education systems regarding language variation affect school structures and practices. Indeed, in her discussion of deficit constructions of Māori children in New Zealand schools, Fleur Harris counters deficit discourses through her advocacy for viewing 'Māori children from a post-colonial eye-glass, one that challenges the colonial lens through which Māori children continue to be constructed as deficient learners' (Harris, 2008: 53). Without this change in ideology, Indigenous students in settler schools will continue to be 'recipients of the same old colonial vision parcelled in different terminology' (Harris, 2008: 53).

We have to become more adept at recognizing societal discourses for what they are. Given the influence they hold over generations of students, it is essential that teachers, in particular, learn to recognize such instances as structural and as evidence of 'common sense' discourses that circulate about language and speakers.

It is not effective to simply replace traditional teaching practices without first working to understand and, subsequently, transform the beliefs that produce discriminatory teaching practices. A child's language and behaviour in the classroom influences a teacher's perceptions of the student's potential. The teacher's expectations of the student, in turn, influence his or her pedagogical choices as well as the performance of the child. There is also robust anti-racist and teacher education research that argues that it is through challenging educator positionalities and practices that the cycle of oppression in schools can be disrupted (Hooks, 1994, McIntyre, 1997; Nieto, 1996; Schick, 2000; Schick & St Denis, 2003).

While I believe that schools have a serious role to play in providing access to languages of power (Delpit, 1988), I would argue that educators are not well positioned to fulfil this responsibility if they have low or biased expectations of Indigenous students as the result of their untroubled standard language ideologies. Without making changes to existing language ideologies through the deconstruction of these views; the introduction of alternative discourses; and careful reflection upon the ways in which existing views of language benefit us as settler educators, Indigenous students in settler schools will continue to be 'recipients of the same old colonial vision parcelled in different terminology' (Harris, 2008: 53). Language education that negates indigenized English varieties and positions Indigenous students as less capable of developing reading literacy contributes to the reproduction of the racial hierarchy of white settler societies. Thinking about languages in new ways means moving towards de-colonizing our thinking about the past and present and challenging our assumptions about ourselves, Others and 'standards' of language.

7 'Radical Solutions' for Schools and Teacher Education

Introduction

As I explained in the introductory chapter, the goals of this book are to (a) to develop awareness of the colonial past and its present-day influences on settler schools; (b) to take a close look at the effects of present-day settler nationalism on constructions of race and language in settler schools; and (c) to explore what could be done differently to lessen present-day and future educational inequity. In working towards these goals, the research described in this book has been carried out in the context of a settler society and explored the complex dynamics, relationships and systems that are engendered by the history of such a place. I have drawn on the frameworks of postcolonial theory and critical race theory so as to ground this book's discussions both socially and historically. This final chapter (a) provides a synthesis of these ideas as well as the research presented throughout this book and (b) builds on this synthesis as I explore possible implications of this research for schools, pre-service teaching programmes and future research in this field.

Review of Main Arguments

Let me begin by providing a brief summary and synthesis of this book's main arguments. I have argued that schools and educator views of language are historically and socially located; that schools and communities are racialized spaces, as are the people who live, study and work within them, and that what constitutes proper English is a colonial invention but that this view of English, as constructed as it is, has some very real effects on literacy education. With these arguments in mind, I maintain that in order to understand the complexities of these issues, it is necessary to move towards a critical approach to examining language variation in educational research, one that considers issues such as colonial history, racial identity and the institutional systems of settler nations which serve to reproduce racial and linguistic hierarchies. Simply focusing on attitudes of educators, pedagogical practices or linguistic awareness of teachers is an overly localized focus. Examinations of language variation in settler societies can be enriched by a historical and societal understanding of the systems that inform the patterns around language variation in settler schools.

In the settler context that informs this book, this critical approach to understanding language variation means that it is necessary to consider how empire-building and settler nationalism influence views of linguistic alterity in settler schools. It also means considering the continued influence of colonial discourses on what gets taught in settler schools as well as how these lessons, in turn, produce the racial identities of students. Through this consideration, we can come to understand the roles that schools play in reproducing dominance. Also of importance is developing an understanding of schools as white spaces as well as all this racialization of space implies for those who educate and learn within it.

Colonial discourses act upon teacher identities and the pedagogical choices they make. These influences can be seen in terms of how teachers position students as legitimate or illegitimate speakers of English. When interviewed, white settler, Métis and First Nations educators all demonstrate awareness of Indigenous English but it would appear that the discursive effects of standard language cultures are at play. None of the educators involved in this research were familiar with the idea of multiple Englishes or the possible inclusion of other Englishes in school activities. As such, educators, First Nations and white settlers, who are helping students to build fluency in the written norms of prestige English, are doing so by trial and error or drawing on previous personal experiences. These pedagogical choices, as ad hoc as they might be, need to be recognized as alternatives to choices influenced by standard language discourses.

In this study, some white settler educators discussed First Nations and Métis students as operating with a language deficit or with language delays. I suggest that limited awareness of language variation among educators, combined with biased perceptions of speech and lowered expectations of Indigenous English-speaking children, leads to ineffective teaching practices contributing to literacy development difficulties for First Nations and Métis students. Improvements in the students' test results, combined with Deborah's success in improving her students' literacy abilities, lend support to my position regarding educator bias.

Drawing on an understanding of colonial history, settler nationalism and the role that schools play in producing race and dominance allows for a more critical analysis of the language views of teachers in this study. By providing a macro-analysis of this particular settler context, the views of

Indigenized English and what this variety implies for a student's perceived ability to develop literacy skills, allows for practices such as speech and language referrals; literacy programmes that overemphasize phonics; deficit discourses about students' language and vocabulary; and 'pull-outs' from regular classrooms to be understood through a colonial lens. These types of routinized practices that have come to seem 'normal' and 'everyday' in schools where children like Crystal study need to be carefully considered. Are they really the only options available? Are children benefitting from these solutions? Or, instead, are these routine events examples of Indigenous students being discursively constructed as illegitimate speakers of English? Are educators involved in the colonial pattern of suppressing alterity in others?

It would seem that many educators continue to see English language variation in a fixed and nationalist way. Through this lens, language differences are pathologized and so, then, are the humans who produce them. This book suggests that there are other options available to us in terms of how we think about performances of English in settler schools. As an educational community, we need to remove the colonialist lens we have employed for centuries in firmly fixing our gaze on the Other and the Other's use of language. It is important to consider what is gained by positioning indigenized language varieties and their speakers in this way. I suggest that it is necessary to consider historical processes such as colonialism in our attempts to understand language variation for what they may actually be: a performance of postcolonial identities and a form of resistance to the hegemony of 'standard' languages. Using this postcolonial lens is increasingly critical in light of the times in which we now live. Settler schools can no longer afford to promote national forms of languages and literacies to the exclusion of others. Given the nature of globalization, language variation and intercultural communication skills of Indigenous students need to be seen in a positive light and acknowledged for the valuable linguistic resources they bring with them to educational fields. Knowing how to play with language in creative and new ways and to seamlessly adapt to interlocutor's differences are abilities that schools need to recognize and cultivate.

Implications for Schools, Teacher Education and Future Research

In this final section, I want to discuss what the research presented in this book can tell us about the role of the teacher, teacher educator and educational researcher involved in working with speakers of indigenized Englishes in settler schools. Specifically, I will provide some suggestions for teachers and teacher educators and discuss implications for future research. Not all the suggestions that I make in this chapter will be pertinent to every settler school context. It is important, then, for readers to focus on those recommendations that seem relevant to their own context. What works in Saskatchewan, for example, in terms of how this province structures professional development possibilities or curricular reform might not transfer to an educational context in New Zealand.

Let me begin, then, with a list of suggestions for teachers and teacher educators who are critically aware of how they are situated and wish to work towards creating equitable educational experiences for students who are speakers of indigenized (and othered) Englishes:

Critical awareness

As I have suggested throughout this book, critical awareness of how colonial discourses continue to shape the lived experiences of teachers and students is an important first step. Given the role of teacher identity can play in producing educational inequity, teachers need to be aware of how their identities can potentially influence pedagogical choices. It is important to remember that this process is ongoing and involves regular self-reflection. Corson also suggests that 'one way for beginning teachers to become critically aware of non-standard and standard issues, would be for them to study the critical practices of critical practitioners themselves: to look at other teachers who have managed to put themselves inside these issues, and then used that awareness to reconstruct the education they offer' (Corson, 2001).

For teacher educators, it is likely important to begin from a point which acknowledges that helping pre-service teachers move towards critical awareness cannot be achieved without helping them to engage with their feelings and experiences. This understanding grows out of the field of critical pedagogy and the work of Paulo Freire (1970). Freire made many contributions to educational study; one of his concepts that I will draw on here is an understanding of 'critical consciousness'. At one end of the critical consciousness spectrum, you might find students who are unable to see that humans can change their lives or society. A student with little critical consciousness accepts the status quo as 'normal' and sees themselves as disconnected and without influence on systems of power. A student at the other end of the spectrum, or someone who is critically conscious or aware, would be more able to perceive connections between 'individual experience and social issues, between single problems and the larger social system' (Shor, 1992: 127).

Unless pre-service students learn to see the connections between biased school practices and the colonial past, racial hierarchy of the present and the social inequities between settlers and Indigenous peoples in settler societies, it is likely that they will replicate these same biased teaching practices when they become members of a school community and encounter the dominant standard language discourses that circulate. In light of this reality, it is important to help them make these links through their courses and the types of reflective projects assigned. For any number of factors (personal experiences, family experiences and friends, to name a few) some students are resistant to the idea of linguistic diversity and others are more receptive to learning in order to see language, schools and society in new ways.

In terms of how settler identities may impact on views of linguistic difference there are several considerations. Corson suggests that 'a most important thing teachers can do in this regard is to think about their own discourse norms, then ask themselves whether culturally different children are receiving unintended messages of domination, exclusion, or hostility from the way they interact with their students themselves' (Corson, 2001: 64). When interacting with children who are linguistically different from themselves, teachers can ask themselves the following questions: Do I feel resentful of this student's linguistic difference (accent, grammar, code-switching, differences in discourse behaviour)? Am I simply frustrated by communication breakdown? Is there something I can do to positively influence our interaction? Am I making any judgements or assumptions about this student's character, family, background or potential for academic achievement based on some aspect of their linguistic performance? Am I pathologizing aspects of this student's speech or language? Feelings of resentment or judgement might signal a need for reflection. Once teachers have begun the work of becoming critically aware of how they are situated, they are better placed to assist their own students in their literacy development.

Linguistic knowledge

There is research to indicate that teacher linguistic bias can be influenced by the introduction of 'linguistic knowledge' or 'dialect awareness' (Abdul-Hakim, 2002; Blake & Cutler, 2003; Bundgens-Koshen, 2009; Patton, 2008). What this means for teachers is that learning more about: linguistic diversity; features of Englishes and language variation has the potential to positively influence their views of other Englishes. In terms of pre-service teacher education programmes, it seems wise to focus on including language variation awareness content in required literacy and language arts courses. In this way, new teachers can receive awareness training at the university level that should contribute to dispelling dangerous biases towards students' language and discourse behaviour. In turn, their increased awareness could help in terms of countering nationalist discourses about legitimate languages. This work also needs to be linked to the larger historical context in which language variation occurs.

For those in-service teachers who are unable to access courses in 'dialects and education' or 'linguistic diversity and education', books and websites can be good sources of information. A number of books I mentioned in Chapter 2 could be useful in this regard: Shondel Nero's (2006a) edited volume includes explorations of many English language varieties and creoles (e.g. beyond simply African American English) including Caribbean, Hawaiian, African and Asian Englishes. Walt Wolfram, Carolyn Temple Adger and Donna Christian's well-known 1999 monograph explores English variation in the United States and provides readers with research-based pedagogical tools and materials.

Increasing linguistic flexibility

Canagarajah views the ability to interpret 'the meanings of words from diverse varieties' of English as the 'cultural capital of multilingual people, developed through history. Monolinguals fail to develop these resources as they assume the need for similarity in order to enable communication' (Canagarajah, 2007: 237). Speaking about learners of English, Canagarajah makes the following statement:

> We have to develop negotiation strategies among our students. We have to train them to assume difference in communication and orientate them to sociolinguistic and psychological resources that will enable them to navigate sociolinguistic difference. This means that we have to move away from an obsession with correctness. Correctness usually assumes the existence of a common/legitimate core of grammar. (Canagarajah, 2007: 237)

The responsibility for successful communication should be shared across interlocutors. This means that accommodation or adaptation in intercultural communication should not fall to speakers of indigenized or othered Englishes; teachers also have responsibility to add to their own linguistic resources. Consider the following story shared by Carmen Chacón:

> One of the first things most people notice when I speak English is my accent. It is not uncommon for me to hear the questions, 'Where are you from?' 'Are you Mexican?' I am used to comments like 'Your accent sounds nice.' During my second journey as a graduate student in the

United States, I got used to hearing the phrase 'Can you say that again?' Often, some people looked at me in a puzzled way, without saying a word, which made me feel worse than I did when having to repeat things to make myself understood. Many times, I thought to myself, 'this person has a monolingual ear.' For me, a monolingual ear means somebody who belongs to a homogenous group affiliation, and who is not used to diversity or who is not willing to understand accents other than his or her own – or the so- called 'Standard American English'. (Chacón, 2006: 56)

I think there are two things that can be done to improve a 'monolingual ear' or increase flexibility in the linguistic systems of teachers. There is research that demonstrates that becoming familiar with accents will help to overcome negative expectations of interlocutors who sound different from ourselves (Derwing *et al.*, 2002; Gass & Varonis, 1984; Rubin, 1992). Spending time around speakers of other Englishes can help in this regard as well as help teachers to develop linguistic awareness about vocabulary, verb and sentence structure differences across varieties of English. It is also likely important to pay specific attention to differences between students' speech communities and the prestige English targeted in schools.

The second suggestion I make is that monolingual teachers consider working towards developing fluency in a second language. Acquiring additional languages can have the effect of broadening one's experience of language and the world. Linguistic difference has the potential to seem 'normal' after having experienced language learning. In addition to working towards increased linguistic flexibility among educators, I also believe this should be considered in educational programming for students. I discuss this more in the forthcoming section on curriculum.

Referrals

One of the reasons that the previous three suggestions are important is because teachers who have developed critical awareness of colonial discourses and their influence on educator views of language; who have increased their linguistic knowledge; and who are linguistically flexible will be better equipped to make fair and unbiased assessment referrals of Indigenous students to speech and language practitioners. One of the findings of this study was that a disproportionate number of First Nations and Métis students appeared to have been referred for language and speech assessment by their classroom teachers. Biased assessment can result in misdiagnosis of speech, language and learning difficulties, which, in turn, can potentially further exacerbate students' attempts to develop literacy skills in mainstream classrooms (Harris, 1985). It is important to be sure that referrals are actually needed and not just a response to children performing English in indigenized ways. Teachers who are not sure as to whether a particular feature or pattern of a child's speech or language is a cause for referral should consider consulting with adult members of the child's speech community: other teachers, speech and language professionals, teacher assistants, parents and community members.

Testing

It is important, whenever possible, to avoid testing procedures that favour the prestige or settler variety of English. In reality, these tests often simply reflect student knowledge of the prestige or settler English variety and tell us little about genuine ability. In many cases, however, teachers do not have the choice to determine which tests will be used in their classrooms. Often, these decisions are made at the school, school board or provincial (state) level. It is unlikely that any test can be culturally or linguistically neutral but for those teachers who are required to administrator tests of sight words or reading ability, it may be possible to affect the bias of the exams in some small ways. One of the things that Deborah and I discussed was the topic of 'reading miscues' during tests of students' reading ability. Deborah wondered if she evaluated 'miscues' in her students in the same way that someone from a settler discourse community might. Deborah believed that, in some cases, teachers in previous grades might have scored students' pronunciation of certain words as 'reading miscues', whereas she might simply hear her students' pronunciation as 'normal' or another possible pronunciation. One example we discussed was the word 'there' being pronounced as 'der' by some of her First Nations students when reading. She chose not to score this as a reading miscue. Here is an example where informed teachers might choose to consider Deborah's example.

Curriculum

The increased mingling of multiple Englishes in Canadian schools (as the result of present linguistic pluralism as well as increased immigration) has implications for how to teach language and literacies curriculum. There are several ways that teachers can work towards presenting pluralistic views of language and communication in their own classrooms. Educators should strive to frame classroom discussions of language norms, history and society in critical ways. Teachers, particularly those in settler societies, need to learn to talk about racial inequity and linguistic difference so that they can help their students to notice normative discourses about race and language. These types of conversations might take the form of asking children to make sense of why we hear particular languages in certain spaces.

Dagenais *et al.* draw on linguistic landscape theory to investigate 'how children imagine the languages of their neighbourhoods and construct their identities in relation to them' (Dagenais *et al.*, 2009: 254). Students involved in their studies participate in activities that 'aim at having students explore several languages in class to develop an appreciation of linguistic diversity. Students participate in discussions about multilingualism, manipulate texts, listen to audio recordings, and watch video clips in a range of languages, many of which they have not previously heard' (Dagenais *et al.*, 2009: 258). The students discuss patterns between languages, attribute meaning to the new languages they have heard, discuss how languages are valued and devalued in their communities and they also spend time discussing the stereotyping of speakers of particular languages. Later, students learn to document their linguistic landscapes by photographing 'literacy cues' in their schools and communities. The authors suggest that the practices included in their study provide 'a promising avenue for teaching about language diversity and literacy perspectives from a critical perspective' (Dagenais *et al.*, 2009: 266). In addition to the practices discussed in this study of linguistic landscaping, language diversity can also be introduced to students by exposing them to multiple Englishes (through teachers, educational staff, videos, visitors and volunteers, Youtube; video penpals) and explicitly learning receptive knowledge or at least awareness of lexicon, morphology, syntax and discourse behaviour in other Englishes. These practices have the potential to lead to increased linguistic flexibility in students.

Make things explicit

Finally, I want to include with a suggestion informed by the writings of Lisa Delpit (1988). Delpit suggests the following about the 'culture or power' found in schools (and other institutions):

(1) Issues of power are enacted in classrooms.
(2) There are codes or rules for participating in power, that is, there is a 'culture of power'.
(3) The rules of the culture of power are a reflection of the rules of the culture of those who have power.
(4) If you are not already a participant in the culture of power, being told explicitly the rules of that culture makes acquiring power easier.

(5) Those with power are frequently least aware of – or least willing to acknowledge – its existence. Those with less power are often most aware of its existence (Delpit, 1988: 282).

It is point (4) from Delpit's list that I want to consider in connection to how teachers interact with students who are speakers of indigenized or othered Englishes. What I suggest in this book is that schools and teachers need to respond differently to language variation. In addition to introducing more pluralistic, inclusive and postcolonial views of English, schools and teachers continue to have the responsibility to prepare students for societies where colonial discourses about languages continue to circulate. In order to access the 'culture of power', children who are speakers of Indigenous English also need to be explicitly taught the rules of settler English so that they are able to 'participate in power'.

Drawing on classroom practices of teachers involved in my research, I suggest that two pedagogical interventions can be effective towards this end: corrective feedback (Lyster & Ranta, 1997) and contrastive analysis (Rickford, 2006). I observed both of these methods being successfully used in the school where I conducted my research. The first intervention is related to something called 'corrective feedback' in second language education research. Corrective feedback refers to information given to students by their teachers about 'errors' or, in this case, the features of their Englishes that are not features of the written English targeted in schools. Roy Lyster and Leila Ranta's (1997) study of teacher feedback was conducted in Canadian French immersion classrooms and found that there are six ways of giving feedback. In this study of teacher responses towards the 'errors' made by second language learners of French, there is an overwhelming tendency for teachers to use 'recasts' in spite of this feedback move's ineffectiveness at leading to changes in learners' language. This type of feedback move might appear somewhat like the following:

Student: I seen four cats last night
Teacher: Oh, you saw four cats last night. You're lucky!

The danger here is that the teacher's correction can be perceived by the student to be a continuation of topic or simply another possible form of the verb 'to see'. This feedback move is potentially too implicit for students to notice. Four other feedback types – elicitation, metalinguistic feedback, clarification requests and repetition – have the potential to lead to students being able to notice and self-repair. In these moves, learners are made aware of the non-target-like form through tone, pausing and information about language (i.e. you are missing a verb in your sentence). These more explicit moves help students to know that there's a change needed in their written language. Lyster and Ranta suggest that it is by noticing 'errors' and through self-repair that these target forms of language can eventually become part of students' language.

What is important to know about corrective feedback is that the more explicit a teacher is in pointing out the learners' non-target-like form (but not providing the correction for the student), the easier it is for the learner to (a) notice that they have received some feedback about a non-target-like form and (b) then attempt to self-repair. I saw Deborah explicitly telling students when they used forms of written English that did not comply with conventional rules. She did not provide students with the target form; she simply asked something along the lines of 'is that how you say that when you're writing' and some of the time this lead to a child making a change in the written form. Sometimes she did have to help them with the correct form but nothing about the exchange was implicit or open for interpretation. The students knew there were rules of writing that needed to be attended to and Deborah explicitly told them when they did not.

The second pedagogical intervention that I suggest teachers consider using in their interactions with students who are speakers of indigenized Englishes is what Rickford (2006) refers to as contrastive analysis. Proponents of this approach suggest that fluency in the target English language variety can only be achieved by teaching students to identify and explore differences through classroom activities (Delpit, 1988; Fogel & Ehri, 2000; Pandey, 2000; Rickford, 2006; Rickford & Rickford, 1995; Wolfram et al., 1999). Rickford maintains that this approach uses student fluency in their first language variety as a 'springboard' for developing fluency in the prestige variety valued by schools; in this way, it 'proceeds from a position of strength' (Rickford, 2006: 83). Rickford (2006) also argues that this approach allows teachers to systematically target problem areas for students which allows for increased efficiency in the classroom. In my study, Rachel described using this approach with her Grade 8 students and found it to be effective in helping them to make sense of similarities and difference between their Englishes and the prestige forms of English expected in their written texts. If teachers do want to make use of this particular approach, they need to develop a well-informed understanding of the features of their students' Englishes. This can be achieved through observation, through discussion with adults from the students' speech communities and by analysing the forms of English in their students' written work. Developing this sort of understanding of students' English will help teachers to understand which features they may wish to target in their lessons.

The above-described suggestions are directed to those teachers and teacher educators who are interested in building on ideas presented in this book in terms of their classroom practices. Before I move on to a discussion of potential implications of this study for future research, let me make one suggestion for school administrators. One of the findings of my study is that school practices that systematically marginalize Indigenous students can be countered by the presence of Indigenous teachers. As such, I would recommend increasing the presence of Indigenous teachers and support staff in settler schools. Corson also advocates an increase in 'teachers from appropriate cultural backgrounds entering classrooms that cater for diverse students' (Corson, 2001: 96). School boards may wish to actively recruit applications from Indigenous pre-service teachers and, indeed, many already do so. My study also revealed, however, that Indigenous educators teaching experiences in Saskatchewan schools can be isolating and difficult for a number of reasons including the racialization of urban and school spaces. As such, it is important to provide these educators with the support they need to do their important work. This support could take a number of formats and could include meetings with school administrators, peer mentors and support groups within the school or in conjunction with other schools. I think it is also important, in light of my study's findings regarding schools as white spaces, that settler teachers be involved in these discussions. Because racial spatialization largely affects us in positive ways, we have to work hard to understand that the spaces we live in can be experienced very differently by bodies that are not white. I think much work needs to be done to help move settler teachers towards a more critical understanding of this reality so that Indigenous teachers like Deborah in my study can be better supported by other educators.

In terms of possible future studies, a number of possibilities come to mind as a result of the findings revealed by this study. First, there is the possibility for future linguistic studies of Indigenized Englishes. Better understanding the characteristics of these varieties of English could lead to the creation of improved and varied pedagogical tools, for example, language readiness tests and contrastive analysis programmes. Another possible implication for future research might be an intervention study which introduces a literacy programme that includes additional steps for speakers of indigenized Englishes. Such programmes are used with in countries such as the United States and Australia. Examining the effects of a bridging programme could be of interest to researchers and educators. Another possible study could make use of participatory action research methods with educators. This type of research could be used to address and counter language biases or to examine the experiences of First Nations and Métis educators in Saskatchewan schools. Both options could provide insight into practices and policies that are indicative of institutional racism.

I would like to also appeal to researchers in the field of speech and language pathology. During my doctoral studies, I was fortunate enough to study language acquisition in a multidisciplinary programme alongside linguists, speech and language pathologists and doctoral students in psychology. Learning to understand language from multiple perspectives was a rich learning experience for me and one thing I took away was a great appreciation for the rigour and technique that speech and language pathologists bring to the study of language. There is a particularly pressing need for the application of this rigour and technique in terms of properly normed assessment tools and the development and implementation of language assessment tests. We cannot continue to assess the speech and language needs of students in heterogeneous settler societies in homogeneous ways. A recent article written by Sharla Peltier, an Aboriginal speech-language pathologist, discusses promising therapeutic practices for use with Indigenous students who speak varieties of Indigenous Englishes (Peltier, 2011).

The suggestions for teachers and teacher educators and the suggestions for future studies described here are only some of the possibilities of this field. It is my hope that some of these ideas, and others that I have not considered, can contribute to improving the school experiences of speakers of indigenized varieties of languages students in settler schools. Yet, Dixon and Rousseau maintain that the call to action through 'recommendations for changes in educational policy and practice' is but a first step in moving towards the types of 'radical solutions' first proposed by Ladson-Billings (1994) and argue that too often, we fail as educators to mobilize and move beyond the proposal of 'mere recommendations' (Dixon & Rousseau, 2005: 23). My intention, then, in writing this book has been to spur educators, educational researchers, and teacher educators towards the types of 'radical solutions' that have the potential to 'address the persistent and pernicious educational inequity' found in settler schools like the one I have profiled in this book (Dixon & Rousseau, 2005: 23).

References

Aaron, R. and Powell, G. (1982) Feedback practices as a function of teacher and pupil race during reading group interaction. *Journal of Negro Education* 51, 50–59.
Abdul-Hakim, I. (2002) Florida preservice teachers' attitudes toward African American vernacular English. PhD thesis, Florida State University. etd.lib.fsu.edu/theses/available/etd-06232003-112932/
Abernethy, D.B. (2000) *The Dynamics of Global Dominance: European Overseas Empires 1415–1980*. New Haven, CT: Yale University Press.
Absolon, K. and Willett, C. (2004) Aboriginal research: Berry picking and hunting in the 21st century. *First Peoples Child and Family Review* 1, 5–17.
Adams, H. (1989) *Prison of Grass: Canada from a Native Point of View*. Saskatoon, SK: Fifth House Publishers.
Adams, H. (1999) *Tortured People: The Politics of Colonization*. Penticton, BC: Theytus Books Ltd.
Alfred, T. (1999) *Peace, Power, Righteousness: An Indigenous Manifesto*. Oxford: Oxford University Press.
Alfred, T. and Corntassel, J. (2005) Being indigenous: Resurgences against contemporary colonialism. *Government and Opposition* 40, 597–614.
Amin, N. (1999) Minority women teachers of ESL: Negotiating white English. In G. Braine (ed.) *Non-native Educators in English Language Teaching* (pp. 93–104). New Jersey: Lawerence Erlbaum.
Anderson, B. (1983) *Imagined Communities*. London: Verso.
Andreotti, V. (2007) An ethical engagement with the other: Spivak's ideas on education. *Critical Literacy: Theories and Practices* 1, 69–79.
Arthur, J.M. (1996) *Aboriginal English: A Cultural Study*. Melbourne, VIC: Oxford University Press.
Ashcroft, T. (2001) *Post-Colonial Transformation*. New York: Routledge.
Atleo, E.R. (2004) *Tsawalk: A Nuu-chah-nulth Worldview*. Vancouver, BC: University of British Columbia Press.
Battiste, M. (ed.) (2000) *Reclaiming Indigenous Voice and Vision*. Vancouver, BC: University of British Columbia Press.
Baugh, J. (1983) *Black Street Speech: Its History, Structure and Survival*. Austin, TX: University of Texas Press.
Berlin, J.A. (1987) *Rhetoric and Reality: Writing Instruction in American Colleges, 1900–1985*. Carbondale, IL: SIU Press.
Bex, T. and Watts, R.J. (1999) *Standard English: The Widening Debate*. London: Routledge.
Bhabha, H.K. (ed.) (1990) *Nation and Narration*. London, New York: Routledge.
Blake, M. and Van Sickle, M. (2001) Helping linguistically diverse students share what they know. *Journal of Adolescent and Adult Literacy* 44, 468–475.
Blake, R. and Cutler, C. (2003) AAE and variation in teachers' attitudes: A question of school philosophy? *Linguistics and Education* 14, 163–194.

Bourdieu, P. (1991) *Language and Symbolic Power.* Cambridge: Polity Press.
Brice-Heath, S. (1983) *Ways with Words: Language, Life, and Work in Communities and Classrooms.* New York: Cambridge University Press.
Brodkey, L. (1994) Writing on the bias. *College English* 56, 527–547.
Brodkey, L. (1996) I site. *Open Letter* 6, 17–30.
Bumsted, J.M. (2001) *Louis Riel v. Canada: The Making of a Rebel.* Winnipeg, MB: Great Plains Publications.
Bündgens-Kosten, J. (2009) Teachers' attitudes toward African American vernacular English: Influence of contact with linguistics on ambivalent attitudes. PhD thesis, RWTH Aachen University. Online document: http://darwin.bth.rwth-aachen.de/opus/volltexte/2009/2936/. Last accessed on 18.8.11.
Cajete, G. (2000) Indigenous knowledge: The Pueblo metaphor of Indigenous education. In M. Battiste (ed.) *Reclaiming Indigenous Voice and Vision* (pp. 181–191). Vancouver, BC: University of British Columbia Press.
Canagarajah, A.S. (1999) *Resisting Linguistic Imperialism in English Teaching.* Oxford: Oxford University Press.
Canagarajah, A.S. (2007) After disvention: Possibilities for communication, community, and competence. In S. Makoni and A. Pennycook (eds) *Disventing and Reconstituting Languages* (pp. 233–239). Clevedon: Multilingual Matters.
Canagarajah, A.S. (2008) Foreword. In A. Clemente and M. Higgins (eds) *Performing English with a Postcolonial Accent: Ethnographic Narratives from Mexico* (pp. ix–xiii). London: The Tufnell Press.
Cazden, C. (1988) *Classroom Discourse: The Language of Teaching and Learning.* Portsmouth, NH: Heinemann.
Cecil, N. (1988) Black dialect and academic success: A study of teacher expectations. *Reading Improvement* 25, 34–38.
Chacón, C. (2006) My journey into racial awareness. In A. Curtis and M. Romney (eds) *Color, Race, and English Language Teaching: Shades of Meaning* (pp. 49–64). Mahwah, NJ: Lawrence Erlbaum Associates.
Chamberlain, M. (2008) PIRLS 2005/2006 in New Zealand: An overview of national findings from the second cycle of the Progress in International Reading Literacy Study (PIRLS). Online document: http://www.educationcounts.govt.nz/publications/series/2539/pirls_0506/34905/34906.
Clemente, A. and Higgins, M. (2008) *Performing English with a Postcolonial Accent: Ethnographic Narratives from Mexico.* London: The Tufnell Press.
Cohen, E.G. and Lotan, R. (2004) Equity in heterogeneous classrooms. In J. Banks and C. Banks (eds) *Handbook for Multicultural Education* (2nd edn) (pp. 736–750). San Francisco, CA: Jossey-Bass/Wiley.
Commission of Inquiry into Matters Related to the Death of Neil Stonechild (2004) Final report. Online document: www.stonechildinquiry.ca/finalreport/default.shtml. Last accessed on 18.8.11.
Corson, D. (2001) *Language Diversity and Education.* Mahwah, NJ: Lawrence Erlbaum Associates.
Correctional Service of Canada (2008) Aboriginal offenders and incarceration. Online document: www.csc-scc.gc.ca/text/pblct/sexoffender/aboriginal/aboriginale-03_e.shtml
Covington, A.J. (1975) Teacher's attitudes toward Black English: Effects on student achievement. In R.L. Williams (ed.) *Ebonics: The True Language of Black Folks* (pp. 40–54). St Louis: Institute for Black Studies.

Crago, M. (1992) Communicative interaction and second language acquisition: An Inuit example. *TESOL Quarterly* 26, 489–505.
Crosland Nebeker, K. (1998) Critical race theory: A white graduate student's struggle with this growing area of scholarship. *Qualitative Studies in Education* 11, 25–41.
Crystal, D. (1995) *The Cambridge Encyclopedia of the English Language*. Cambridge: Cambridge University Press.
Cummins, J. (2000) *Language, Power, and Pedagogy: Bilingual Children in the Crossfire*. Clevedon: Multilingual Matters.
Dagenais, D., Moore, D., Lamarre, S., Sabatier, C. and Armand, F. (2009) Linguistic landscape and language awareness. In E. Shohamy and D. Gorter (eds) *Linguistic Landscape: Expanding the Scenery* (pp. 253–269). New York: Routledge/Taylor & Francis Group.
Darnell, R. (1981) Taciturnity in Native American etiquette: A Cree case. *Culture* 1, 55–96.
Dei, G. (1999) The denial of difference: Reframing anti-racist praxis. *Race, Ethnicity and Education* 2, 17–37.
Delgado, R. (ed.) (1995) *Critical Race Theory: The Cutting Edge*. Philadelphia, PA: Temple University.
Delpit, L.D. (1988) The silenced dialogue: Power and pedagogy in educating other people's children. *Harvard Educational Review* 58, 280–298.
Delpit, L. (1995) *Other People's Children: Cultural Conflict in the Classroom*. New York: The New Press.
Delpit, L. (2006) What should teachers do? Ebonics and culturally responsive instruction. In S. Nero (ed.) *Dialects, Englishes, Creoles, and Education* (pp. 93–104). New York: Lawrence Erlbaum Associates.
Delpit, L.D. and Kilgour Dowdy, J. (eds) (2002) *The Skin that We Speak: Thoughts on Language and Culture in the Classroom*. New York: The New Press.
Department of Education, Employment & Workplace Relations (2008) National report to parliament on Indigenous education and training, 2006. Online document: http://www.dest.gov.au/sectors/indigenous_education/publications_resources/other_publications/National_Report_Parliament_Indigenous_2006.htm#publication. Last accessed on 18.8.11.
Derwing, T.M., Rossiter, M.J. and Munro, M.J. (2002) Teaching native speakers to listen to foreign-accented speech. *Journal of Multilingual and Multicultural Development* 23, 245–259.
Deyhle, D. and Swisher, K.G. (1997) Research in American Indian and Alaska native education: From assimilation to self-determination. *Review of Research in Education* 22, 113–194.
Di Giulio, R.C. (1973) Measuring teacher attitudes toward Black English: A pilot project. *The Florida FL Reporter Spring/Fall*, 25–26; 49.
Dixson, A.D. and Rousseau, C.K. (2005) And we are still not saved: Critical race theory in education ten years later. *Race Ethnicity and Education* 8, 7–27.
Eades, D., Jacobs, S., Hargrove, E. and Menacker, T. (2006) Pidgins, local identity, and schooling in Hawai'i. In S. Nero (ed.) *Dialects, Englishes, Creoles, and Education* (pp. 139–163). Mahwah, NJ: Lawrence Erlbaum Associates.
Edwards, J. (2010) *Language Diversity in the Classroom*. Clevedon: Multilingual Matters.
Elbow, P. (2006) Foreword: When the margins are at the center. In S. Nero (ed.) *Dialects, Englishes, Creoles, and Education* (pp. ix–xv). New York: Lawrence Erlbaum Associates.
Eller, R. (1989) Johnny can't talk either: The perpetuation of the deficit theory in classrooms. *Reading Teacher* 42, 670–674.

Epp, R. (2008) *We are All Treaty People. Prairie Essays.* Edmonton, AB: University of Alberta Press.

Farley, A. (1997) The black body as fetish object. *Oregon Law Review* 76 (*Symposium: Citizenship and its Discontents: Centering the Immigrant in the Inter/National Imagination*): 457–535.

Ferrara, N. (1999) *Emotional Expression among Cree Indians: The Role of Pictorial Representations in the Assessment of Psychological Mindedness.* London: Jessica Kingsley Publishers Ltd.

Flores Farfán, J.A. (1999) *Cuatreros somos y toindioma hablamos: contactos y conflictos entre el náhuatl y el español en el sur de México. [We are "cuatreros" and we speak "toindioma": Náhuatl and Spanish contact and conflict in the south of Mexico.]* México: CIESAS.

Fogel, H. and Ehri, L. (2000) Teaching elementary students who speak Black English vernacular to write in standard English: Effects of dialect transformation practice. *Contemporary Educational Psychology* 25, 212–235.

Ford, J.F. (1978) The prospective foreign language teacher and the culturally and linguistically different learner. *Foreign Language Annals* 11, 381–390.

Freire, P. (1970) *Pedagogy of the Oppressed.* New York: Herder and Herder.

Gandhi, L. (1998) *Postcolonial Theory: A Critical Introduction.* New York: Columbia University.

Gass, S. and Varonis, E. (1984) The effect of familiarity on the comprehensibility of non-native speech. *Language Learning* 34, 65–89.

Genee, I. (2010) Blackfoot English dialects in language and literacy education. Paper presented at the Annual Meeting of the Canadian Association of Applied Linguistics, Montreal, Canada.

Godley, A.J., Carpenter, B.D. and Werner, C.A. (2007) "I'll speak in proper slang": Language ideologies in a daily editing activity. *Reading Research Quarterly* 42, 100–131.

Goodman, K.S. and Buck, C. (1973) Dialect barriers to reading comprehension revisited. *Reading Teacher* 27, 6–12.

Government of Saskatchewan (2009) Treaty Land Entitlement: Where Are We Now? Online document: http://www.fnmr.gov.sk.ca/lands/tle/history/5. Last accessed on 18.8.11.

Green, L.J. (2002) *African American English: A Linguistic Introduction.* Cambridge: Cambridge University Press.

Harris, F. (2008) Critical engagement with the historical and contemporary deficit construction of Maori children. *Critical Literacy: Theories and Practices Journal* 2, 43–59.

Harris, G.A. (1985) Considerations in assessing English language performance of Native American children. *Topics in Language Disorders* 5, 42–52.

Heit, M. and Blair, H. (1993) Language needs and characteristics of Saskatchewan Indian and Metis students: Implications for educators. In S. Morris, K. McLeod and M. Danesi (eds) *Aboriginal Languages and Education: The Canadian Experience* (pp. 103–128). Oakville: Mosaic.

Honey, J. (1997) *Language is Power: The Story of Standard English and Its Enemies.* London: Faber & Faber.

Hooks, B. (1994) *Teaching to Transgress. Education as the Practice of Freedom.* London: Routledge.

Hoover, M.R., McNair-Knox, F., Lewis, S.A.R. and Politzer, R.L. (1996) African American English attitude measures for teachers. In R.L. Jones (ed.) *Handbook of Tests and Measurements for Black Populations* (Vol. 1) (pp. 383–259). Hampton, VA: Cobb & Henry Publishers.

Hutcheon, L. (1994) Circling the downspout of empire. *Past the Last Post: Theorizing Post-Colonialism and Post-Modernism*. In B. Ashcroft, G. Griffin and H. Tiffin (eds) *Reader in Post-Colonial Theory* (pp. 130–135). London: Routledge.

Kachru, B. (1992) *The Other Tongue: English across Cultures*. Urbana, IL: University of Illinois Press.

Kamler, B. (2001) *Relocating the Personal: A Critical Writing Pedagogy*. Albany: State University of New York Press.

Kawagley, A.O. (1995) *A Yupiaq World View: A Pathway to Ecology and Spirit*. Prospect Heights, IL: Waveland Press.

Kouritzin, S. (2004) Interpreting the interactions of the "other": Constructing Aboriginal cultures in conversations at and about school. *Journal of Research in Childhood Education* 18, 249–260.

Labov, W. (1972) *Language in the Inner City: Studies in Black English Vernacular*. Philadelphia, PA: University of Pennsylvania Press.

Ladson-Billings, G. (1998) Just what is critical race theory and what's it doing in a nice field like education? *Qualitative Studies in Education* 11, 7–24.

Ladson-Billings, G.J. and Tate, W.F. (1994) Toward a theory of critical race theory in education. *Teachers College Record* 97, 47–68.

Lee, C.D. (2006) Every good-bye ain't gone: Analyzing the cultural underpinnings of classroom talk. *Qualitative Studies in Education* 19, 305–327.

Le Ha, P. (2008) *Teaching English as an International Language: Identity, Resistance and Negotiation*. Clevedon: Multilingual Matters.

Leonardo, Z. (2004) The color of supremacy: Beyond the discourse of "White privilege". *Educational Philosophy and Theory* 36, 137–152.

Little Bear, L. (2000) Jagged worldviews colliding. In M. Battiste (ed.) *Reclaiming Indigenous Voice and Vision* (pp. 77–85). Vancouver, BC: University of British Columbia Press.

Lo Bianco, J. (2000) Multiliteracies and multilingualism. In B. Cope and M. Kalantzis (eds) *Multiliteracies: Literacy Learning and the Design of Social Futures* (pp. 92–105). London: Routledge.

Long, E. and Christensen, J. (1998) Indirect language assessment tool for English-speaking Cherokee Indian children. *Journal of American Indian Education* 38, 1–14.

Loomba, A. (1998) *Colonialism/Postcolonialism: The New Critical Idiom*. London: Routledge.

Lyster, R. and Ranta, L. (1997) Corrective feedback and learner uptake: Negotiation of form in communicative classrooms. *Studies in Second Language Acquisition* 19, 37–66.

Makoni, S. and Pennycook, A. (2005) Disinventing and (re)constituting languages. *Critical Inquiry in Language Studies: An International Journal* 2, 137–156.

Makoni, S. and Pennycook, A. (eds) (2007) *Disventing and Reconstituting Languages*. Clevedon: Multilingual Matters.

Malcolm, I. (1995) Teacher development for bidialectal education. Paper presented at the International Conference on Language in Development, Bali, Indonesia.

Malcolm, I. (2001) Apprehending and appropriating cultural imagery in bidialectal education. *Proceedings of the Annual Meeting of the American Association of Applied Linguistics*, St Louis, pp. 24–27.

Malcolm, I.G. and Sharifian, F. (2002) Aspects of Aboriginal English oral discourse: An application of cultural schema theory. *Discourse Studies* 4, 169–181.

Matsuda, M. (1995) Looking to the bottom: Critical legal studies and reparations. In K. Crenshaw, N. Gotanda, G. Peller and K. Thomas (eds) *Critical Race Theory: The Key Writings that Formed the Movement* (pp. 63–70). New York: The New Press.

McIntyre, A. (1997) *Making Meaning of Whiteness: Exploring Racial Identity with White Teachers*. New York: State University of New York Press.
Mendelson, M. (2004) *Aboriginal People in Canada's Labour Market: Work and Unemployment, Today and Tomorrow*. Ottawa: The Caledon Institute of Social Policy. Online document: http://www.caledoninst.org/Publications/PDF/471ENG.pdf. Last accessed on 18.8.11.
Menezes de Souza, L.M.T. (2002) A Case among Cases, A World among Worlds: The Ecology of Writing among the Kashinawa in Brazil. *Journal of Language, Identity, and Education* 1, 261–278.
Mesthrie, R. and Bhatt, R.M. (2008) *World Englishes: The Study of New Linguistic Varieties*. New York: Cambridge University Press.
Michaels, S. (1981) "Sharing time": Children's narrative styles and differential access to literacy. *Language in Society* 10, 423–442.
Milloy, J. (1999) *A National Crime: The Canadian Government and the Residential School System, 1979 to 1986*. Winnipeg, MB: The University of Manitoba Press.
Milroy, J. (2001) Language ideologies and the consequences of standardization. *Journal of Sociolinguistics* 5/4, 530–555.
Moss, L. (2003) *Is Canada Postcolonial? Unsettling Canadian Literature*. Waterloo, ON: Wilfred Laurier University Press.
Mufwene, S., Rickford, J., Bailey, G. and Baugh, J. (1998) *African-American English: Structure, History and Use*. New York: Routledge.
Nero, S. (ed.) (2006a) *Dialects, Englishes, Creoles, and Education*. Mahwah, NJ: Lawrence Erlbaum Associates.
Nero, S. (2006b) Language, identity, and education of Caribbean English speakers. *World Englishes* 25 (3/4), 501–511.
Nieto, S. (1996) *Affirming Diversity: The Sociopolitical Context of Multicultural Education* (2nd edn). White Plains: Longman.
Pandey, A. (2000) Linguistic power in virtual communities: The Ebonics debate on the internet. *World Englishes* 19, 21–38.
Patton, M.Q. (2008) *Utilization-focused Evaluation* (4th edn). Newbury Park, CA: Sage Publications.
Pavlenko, A. (2002) Poststructuralist approaches to the study of social factors in second language learning and use. In V. Cook (ed.) *Portraits of the L2 User*. Clevedon: Multilingual Matters.
Peltier, S. (2011) Providing culturally sensitive and linguistically appropriate services: An insider construct. *Canadian Journal of Speech-Language Pathology and Audiology* 35 (2), 126–134.
Pennycook, A. (1994) Incommensurable discourses? *Applied Linguistics* 15, 115–138.
Pennycook, A. (1998) *English and the Discourses of Colonialism*. New York: Routledge.
Pennycook, A. (2001) *Critical Applied Linguistics: A Critical Introduction*. Mahwah, NJ: Lawrence Erlbaum Associates.
Pennycook, A. (2003) Beyond homogeny and heterogeny: English as a global and worldly language. In C. Mair (ed.) *The Cultural Politics of English* (pp. 3–17). Amsterdam: Rodopi.
Plank, G. (1994) What silence means for educators of American Indian children. *Journal of American Indian Education* 34, 3–19.
Pratt-Johnson, Y. (2006) Teaching Jamaican Creole-speaking students. In S. Nero (ed.) *Dialects, Englishes, Creoles, and Education* (pp. 119–136). Mahwah, NJ: Lawrence Erlbaum Associates.

Prendergast, C. (2003) *Literacy and Racial Justice: The Politics of Learning After Brown v. Board of Education*. Carbondale, IL: Southern Illinois University Press.
Purcell-Gates, V. (2002) ... As soon as she opened her mouth! In L. Delpit and J.K. Dowdy (eds) *The Skin that We Speak: An Anthology of Essays on Language, Culture and Power* (pp. 121–141). New York: The New Press.
Razack, S. (2002) (ed.) *Race, Space and the Law: Unmapping a White Settler Society*. Toronto, ON: Between the Lines.
Rhodes, V. (2004) First Nations people: Education seen as a key. *The Regina Leader-Post* December 31, p. BB3.
Rickford, J. (1999) *African American English: Features, Evolution, Educational Implications*. Malden, MA: Blackwell.
Rickford, J. (2006) Linguistics, education and the Ebonics firestorm. In S. Nero (ed.) *Dialects, Englishes, Creoles, and Education* (pp. 71–92). New York: Lawrence Erlbaum Associates.
Rickford, R. and Rickford, A. (1995) Dialect readers revisited. *Linguistics and Education* 7, 107–128.
Riley, T. and Ungerleider, C. (2008) Pre-service teachers' discriminatory judgments. *Alberta Journal of Educational Research* 54, 378–387.
Rogers Cherland, M. and Harper, H. (2007) *Advocacy Research in Literacy Education*. Mahwah, NJ: Lawrence Erlbaum Associates.
Roy, J. (1987) The linguistic and sociolinguistic position of Black English and the issue of bidialectism in education. In P. Homel, M. Palif and D. Aaronson (eds) *Childhood Bilingualism: Aspects of Linguistic, Cognitive, and Social Development*. Hillsdale, NJ: Erlbaum Associates.
Rubin, D.L. (1992) Nonlanguage factors affecting undergraduates' judgments of nonnative English-speaking teaching assistants. *Research in Higher Education* 33, 511–531.
Sakoda, K. and Siegel, J. (2003) *Pidgin Grammar: An Introduction to the Creole Language of Hawai'i*. Honolulu, HI: Bess Press.
Saskatchewan Department of Education (1917) *Education of New Canadians*. (Available from Saskatchewan Archives, P.O. Box 1665, Regina, SK, S4P 3C6, 3303 Hillsdale Street, Regina SK, Phone: 306-787-4068, Fax: 306-787-1197, Email: info.regina@archives.gov.sk.ca.)
Saskatchewan Ministry of Education (2008) Saskatchewan Education Indicators Report (2008). Online document: http://www.education.gov.sk.ca/Default.aspx?DN=69222f44-c385-49d7-aff4-9dc770f47750. Last accessed on 18.8.11.
Schick, C. (2000) Keeping the ivory tower white: Discourses of racial domination. *Canadian Journal of Law and Society* 15, 71–90.
Schick, C. (2002) Keeping the ivory tower white: Discourses of racial domination. In S. Razack (ed.) *Race, Space and the Law: Unmapping a White Settler Society* (pp. 100–119). Toronto, ON: Between the Lines.
Schick, C. and St Denis, V. (2003) What makes anti-racist pedagogy in teacher education difficult? Three popular ideological assumptions. *Alberta Journal of Educational Research* 49, 55–69.
Scollon, R. and Scollon, S. (1979) *Linguistic Convergence: An Ethnography of Speaking at Fort Chipewyan, Alberta*. New York: Academic Press.
Scollon, R. and Scollon, S. (1981) *Narrative, Literacy and Face in Interethnic Communication*. Norwood, NJ: Ablex.
Scollon, R. and Scollon, S. (1984) Cooking it up and boiling it down: Abstracts in Athabaskan children's story retellings In D. Tannen (ed.) *Coherence in Spoken and Written Discourse* (pp. 173–197). Norwood, NJ: ABLEX Publishing Corporation.

Seibel Trainor, J. (2005) "My ancestors didn't own slaves": Understanding white talk about race. *Research in the Teaching of English* 40, 140–167.
Sharifian, F. (2001) Schema-based processing in Australian speakers of Aboriginal English. *Language and Intercultural Communication* 1, 120–134.
Sharifian, F. (2006) A cultural-conceptual approach and world Englishes: The case of Aboriginal English. *World Englishes* 25, 11–22.
Sharifian, F. (2008) Aboriginal English in the classroom: An asset or a liability? *Language Awareness* 17, 131–138.
Sharifian, F. (ed.) (2009) *English as an International Language: Perspectives and Pedagogical Issues.* Bristol: Multilingual Matters.
Sharifian, F., Rochecouste, J. and Malcolm, I.G. (2004) "It was all a bit confusing ...": Comprehending Aboriginal English texts. *Language Culture and Curriculum* 17, 203–228.
Shor, I. (1992) *Empowering Education: Critical Teaching for Social Change.* Chicago, IL: University of Chicago Press.
Siegel, J. (2006) Keeping creoles out of the classroom: Is it justified? In S. Nero (ed.) *Dialects, Englishes, Creoles, and Education* (pp. 39–67). Mahwah, NJ: Lawrence Erlbaum Associates.
Siegel, J. (2007) Creoles and minority dialects in education: An update. *Language and Education* 21, 66–86.
Simpson, A. and Erickson, M. (1983) Teachers' verbal and non-verbal communication patterns as a function of teacher race, student gender and student race. *American Education Research Journal* 20, 183–198.
Smith, G. (2000) Protecting and respecting indigenous knowledge. In M. Battiste (ed.) *Reclaiming Indigenous Voice and Vision* (pp. 77–85). Vancouver, BC: University of British Columbia Press.
Smitherman, G. (1977) *Talkin and Testifyin: The Language of Black America.* Boston, MA: Houghton Mifflin.
Smitherman, G. (1991) 'What is Africa to me?': Language, ideology, and African American. *American Speech* 66, 115–132.
Spivak, G. (1990) *The Post-colonial Critic: Interviews, Strategies, Dialogues.* New York: Routledge.
Spivak, G. (1999) *A Critique of Postcolonial Reason: Toward a Critique of the Vanishing Present.* Cambridge, MA: Harvard University Press.
Spolsky, B. (2009) Prolegomena to a sociolinguistic theory of pubic signage. In E. Shohamy and D. Gorter (eds) *Linguistic Landscape: Expanding the Scenery* (pp. 253–269). New York: Routledge.
Stasiulis, D. and Jhappan, R. (1995) The fractious politics of a settler society: Canada. In N. Yuval-Davis and D. Stasiulis (eds) *Unsettling Settler Societies: Articulations of Gender, Race, Ethnicity, and Class* (pp. 95–131). London: Sage Publications.
Stasiulis, D. and Yuval-Davis, M. (eds) (1995) *Unsettling Settler Societies: Articulations of Gender, Race, Ethnicity and Class.* London: Sage Publications.
Statistics Canada (2007) Aboriginal people living off-reserve and the labour market: Estimates from the labour force survey, 2007. Online document: http://www.statcan.gc.ca/pub/71-588-x/2008001/part-partie1-eng.htm. Last accessed on 18.8.11.
Statistics Canada (2008) Literacy profile of off-reserve First Nations and Métis people living in urban Manitoba and Saskatchewan: Results from the International Adult Literacy and Skills Survey 2003. Online document: http://www.statcan.gc.ca/bsolc/olc-cel/olc-cel?lang=eng&catno=81-004-X200700510500. Last accessed on 18.8.11.

Sterzuk, A. (2003) A study of indigenous English speakers in the standard English classroom. Master's thesis, McGill University.
Sterzuk, A. (2008) Whose English counts? Indigenous English in Saskatchewan schools. *McGill Journal of Education* 43, 9–19.
Sterzuk, A. (2009a) Language as an agent of division in Saskatchewan schools. In C. Schick, J. McNinch and L. Comeau (eds) *Challenging the Race and Culture Binary in Education and Service Professions*. Regina, SK: Canadian Plains Research Center.
Sterzuk, A. (2009b) From buffalo plains to wheat fields: Critical thinking in the Canadian Prairies. In A. Churchill (ed.) *Rocking Your World: The Emotional Journey into the Critical Discourses*. Rotterdam, The Netherlands: Sense Publishers.
Sterzuk, A. and Mulholland, V. (2011) Creepy white gaze: Rethinking the diorama as a pedagogical activity. *The Alberta Journal of Education* 57, 1, 16–27.
Taylor, O. (1973) Teachers' attitudes toward Black and nonstandard English as measured by the language attitude scale. In R.W. Shuy and R.W. Fasold (eds) *Language Attitudes: Current Trends and Prospects* (pp. 174–201). Washington, DC: Georgetown University Press.
Thobani, S. (2007) *Exalted Subjects: Studies in the Making of Race and Nation in Canada*. Toronto, ON: University of Toronto Press.
Trudgill, P. (1998) Review of John Honey, language is power: The story of. standard English and its enemies. *Journal of Sociolinguistics* 2, 457–461. http://www.blackwell-synergy.com/doi/pdf/10.1111/1467-9481.00060
Weenie, A. (2000) Post colonial recovering and healing. In J. Reyhner, J. Martin, L. Lockard and W.S. Gilbert (eds) *Learn in Beauty: Indigenous Education for a New Century*. Flagstaff, AZ: Northern Arizona University.
Williams, F. (1973) Some research notes on dialect attitudes and stereotypes. In R.W. Shuy and R. Fasold (eds) *Language Attitudes: Current Trends and Prospects* (pp. 113–128). Washington, DC: Georgetown University Press.
Wiltse, L. (2008) Creating third spaces for minority language learners in a school-university-community research collaboration. Paper presented at the Annual Meeting of the Canadian Society for the Study of Education, Vancouver, Canada.
Winer, L. (2006) Teaching English to Caribbean English Creole-speaking students in the Caribbean and North America. In S. Nero (ed.) *Dialects, Englishes, Creoles, and Education* (pp. 105–118). Mahwah, NJ: Lawrence Erlbaum Associates.
Wolfram, W. and Schilling-Estes, N. (1998) *American English: Dialects and Variation*. Malden, MA: Blackwell.
Wolfram, W., Temple Adger, C. and Christian, D. (1999) *Dialects in Schools and Communities*. Mahwah, NJ: Lawrence Erlbaum Associates.
Woodworth, W.D. and Salzer, R.T. (1971) Black children's speech and teachers' evaluations. *Urban Education* 6, 167–173.

Subject and Author Index

Aboriginal Englishes, 92
Aboriginal Peoples, 5
Academic achievement: see Reading
Academic assessment: see Standardized tests
Adams, Howard, 59, 62, 63, 64, 66, 67
African American Englishes (AAE), 29–30, 92
African American Vernacular English (AAVE): see African American Englishes (AAE)
Alfred, Taiaiake, 60, 61
Algonquian, 16
Algonquian Englishes: see Indigenous English
Alterity, 26, 34, 35, 38, 92
American Indian English: see Indigenous Englishes
Amnesia, postcolonial, 36
Anderson, Benedict, 95–96
Andreotti, Vanessa, 37
Anticolonialism, 2, 7
Australia, 1, 4, 21–23, 32, 37, 51, 55, 92

Batoche, 62–64, 68
Bhabha, Homi, 56
Biculturalism: see common destiny
Bidialectalism: see linguistic flexibility
Black English: see African American Englishes (AAE)
Blackfoot English: see Indigenous Englishes
Blair, Heather, 11, 13, 16, 17, 20, 92
Bourdieu, 8, 46, 92, 93
Brice–Heath, Shirley, 105
British imperialism, 2, 3, 43, 91
British North America Act, 63

Canagarajah, Suresh, 17, 18, 36, 46, 47, 91, 113
Caribbean Creole Englishes, 92
Cartesian philosophy, 34–36, 92
Census Canada, 20, 74
Christian, Donna, 32, 113
Circle of English: see Kachru, Braj
Code-switching, 9, 112: see also Linguistic performance

Subject and Author Index   131

Colonies
  mixed, 51
  occupation, 51
  of exploitation, 1, 51
  plantation, 51
  settler, 1, 51, 52
Colonialism, 1, 2, 4, 35, 36, 43, 45, 48, 51, 57, 72, 91: see also Nationalism, settler
Colour-blindness, 40–43
Common destiny, myth of, 25, 55–56, 59
Contrastive analysis, 30–31, 100, 117–118
Corson, David, 111, 112, 119
Corrective feedback, 117–118
Correctness, 96–97, 113
Counter-history, 26, 59
Cree, 6, 16
Critical applied linguistics, 33, 34, 36
Critical literacy, 3, 7, 39, 47, 86
Critical race theory (CRT), 7, 8, 39–40
Crystal, David, 49
Curriculum, 40, 115

Decolonization, 48
Deconstruction, 37–39, 40, 44, 48
Deficient, 11, 40, 100, 106
Deficit, 23, 29, 38, 43, 93, 98, 99, 105, 106, 110
Delpit, L 30, 31, 32, 93, 105, 107, 116, 117, 118
Denial of difference: see colour-blindness
Descartes, René: see Cartesian philosophy
Dialect, 6–7, 13, 19, 29
Dialect awareness, 31, 112
Dialect interference, 30
Discourse, 46–48
Dixon, Adrienne, 40, 43, 42, 120
Dominance, 4, 5, 15, 68, 70, 73

Ebonics: see African American Englishes (AAE)
Educator linguistic bias, 25, 33
Empire, 45, 51
English as a second dialect (ESD): see linguistic performance
English language variation, 6–7
English language variety: see English language variation
Englishes: see English language variation
Epiphany, linguistic, 32

Epp, Roger, 5, 14, 15, 61, 66
Eurocentric, 50, 68
European imperialism: see Imperialism
Expanding Circle English: see Kachru, Braj

Fairclough, Norman, 46–47
First Nation, 11, 48, 51, 63, 64, 67, 74
First Nations, 6
First Nations English: see Indigenous Englishes
First Peoples, 5
Forgetfulness: see amnesia
Foucault, Michel, 35, 46–47
Foundational fictions, 51, 56, 106
Freire, Paulo, 7, 111

Gandhi, Leela, 35–36
Genocide, 52

Hawai'ian Creole English (Pidgin), 92
Hegemony, 68, 110
Heit, Mary, 11, 13, 16, 17, 20, 92
Hudson's Bay Company, 6, 62
Hypercorrection: see correctness

Ideology, 3, 46–47, 94, 106
Illegitimate, 20, 43, 93, 94
Imperialism, 3, 35, 43, 45, 48, 49, 91, 92
Indian Act, 63
Indian: see First Nations
Indigenous, 5, 6, 20, 22, 35, 51, 52, 66, 67, 92
Indigenous Englishes, 11, 13, 16, 19–20, 91, 92, 100
Indigenous Spanish (Español Indígena), 92
Inner Circle English: see Kachru, Braj
Institutional racism, 71, 60
Intelligence testing: see Standardized test
Inuit, 6
IQ test: see Standardized test

Kachru, Braj, 91

Labov, William, 29, 93, 92
Ladson-Billings, Gloria, 39, 40, 120
Language awareness: see linguistic landscape theory
Language variety, 6–7, 18, 92, 106

Legitimacy, 6, 20, 37, 72, 82, 86, 94, 106, 109, 113
Leonardo, Zeus, 4, 5
Linguistic alterity: see alterity
Linguistic epiphany: see epiphany, linguistic
Linguistic flexibility, 113–114, 116
Linguistic landscape theory, 2, 116
Linguistic othering: see Other
Linguistic performance, 9, 13, 16–18, 20, 56, 91, 110
Linguistic prescriptivism, 91, 96
Literacy, 15, 21, 30, 92, 101, 110
Literacy as white property, 83
Lo Bianco, Joseph, 91
Louis Riel, 62, 64

Makoni, Sinfree, 19, 91
Malcolm, Ian, 31, 92, 93, 105
Métis, 6, 62–64
Milroy, James, 96, 97, 99
Mixed colonies: see colonies
Monolingual ear, 114
Multicultural: see common destiny, myth of
Multiculturalism: see common destiny
Myth of common destiny: see common destiny, myth of

Natal formula, 51
National Policy, 61
Nationalism, settler, 55–56
Native: see First Nations
Native American: see First Nations
Native American English: see Indigenous English
Nero, Shondel, 31, 83, 84, 91, 92, 93, 94, 113
New Zealand, 22, 23, 55, 106
Non-standard English, 6

Occupation colonies: see colonies
Official language variety, 4, 6, 96
Other, 35–37, 55, 66, 70, 77, 83, 92, 93, 110, 113
Othering: see Other
Ottawa, 62–64
Outer Circle English: see Kachru, Braj

Pennycook, Alastair, 2, 19, 33, 34, 36, 46, 47, 91
Performance: see linguistic performance
Pioneer myths, 50
Plantation colonies: see colonies
Portugeuse, Kashiniwa-influenced, 50, 92
Postcolonial rendering: see counter-history
Postcolonial theory, 1, 2, 7, 34, 36, 37, 39, 43, 59, 92
Prendergast, Catherine, 83, 92, 93
Prescriptivism: see linguistic prescriptivism
Print literacy: see literacy
Print-capitalism, 95–96, 106
Proper English, 44, 95, 106, 108
Purcell-Gates, Victoria, 105

Queen's English: see Proper English

Race, 38, 39, 41, 42, 59, 73, 98
Racial hierarchy, 3, 4, 55
Racism, 5, 39, 43, 59
Razack, Sherene, 3, 4, 36, 37, 48, 59, 70, 72, 73, 74, 75, 77, 88
RCMP: see Royal Northwest Mounted Police
Reading
  assessment, 115
  in a second dialect, 30–31
  instruction, 101–103
  statistics for Indigenous students in settler societies, 20–23
Red River Rebellion: see Red River Resistance
Red River Resistance, 62–63
Regina, 59, 60, 63, 67, 74
Repression, 55
Reserve: see First Nation
Residential schools, 65
Riel, Louis: see Louis Riel
Riel Rebellion: see Riel Resistance
Riel Resistance, 62, 64
Royal Northwest Mounted Police, 63

Saskatoon, 59, 60, 74
Saulteaux, 6
Schick, Carol, 41, 42, 69, 70, 82, 107
Schilling-Estes, Natalie, 30

Segregation, 77, 78
Self, 34, 35, 36, 38, 92
Settler, 4
Settler colony: *see* colonies
Settler English: 7, 16–20, 115, 117
Settler mythology, 4, 50, 55, 56, 69
Settler nationalism: *see* Nationalism, settler
Settler postcolonial context, 1, 2
Settler society: *see* white settler society
Sharifian, Farzad, 31, 91, 92
Siegel, Jeff, 31, 32, 92
Social capital, 8
Spatialization, 72–79
Speech and language assessment, 102, 110, 114, 115, 120
Spivak, Gayatri, 36–37
Standard English, 6, 20: *see also* Standard language culture
Standard language culture, 94–98
Standard language discourse, 93–95, 106
Standardized test, 31, 40, 102
Standardization of language, 95–96
Stasiulis, Daiva, 2, 51, 52, 55, 56
Statistics Canada, 21, 75
Sterzuk, Andrea, 50, 68, 92, 93
St-Denis, Verna, 42, 69, 70, 107
Stonechild, Neil, 60
Subjugation, 52, 63, 67

Teacher education, 70, 107, 110–119
Temple Adger, Carolyn, 32, 113
Terra nullius, 50, 71, 72, 94
Text, 46–48
Theory, critical race: *see* Critical Race Theory (CRT)
Theory, postcolonial: *see* Postcolonial theory
Thobani, Sunera, 3, 49, 50, 52, 55, 56, 59, 69
Tolerance, 59: *see also* Common destiny, myth of

Unmapping, 73–74

Western cognitive imperialism, 35
White settler, 4, 5, 8, 15, 41, 56, 68, 70
White settler society, 2–4, 36, 70, 72, 73
White space, 76, 77, 82, 84, 86
White supremacy, 38
White talk, 15
Whiteness, 40, 42–43, 69, 70, 82, 86
Winer, L 92
Winnipeg, 59, 74
Wolfram, Walt, 30, 32, 93, 105, 113, 118
Writing, 93, 100, 101, 117–118

Yuval-Davis, Nira, 2, 51, 55, 56

For Product Safety Concerns and Information please contact our EU Authorised Representative:

Easy Access System Europe

Mustamäe tee 50

10621 Tallinn

Estonia

gpsr.requests@easproject.com